T0086669

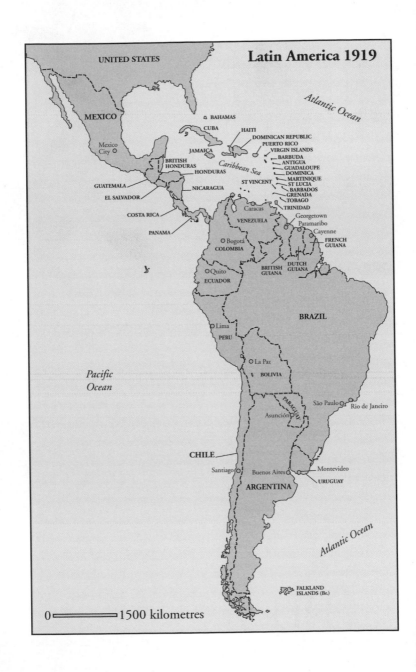

South America

Makers
of the
Modern
World

South America

Michael Streeter

HAUS HISTORIES

First published in Great Britain in 2010 by
Haus Publishing Ltd
70 Cadogan Place
London SW1X 9AH
www.hauspublishing.com

Copyright © Michael Streeter, 2010

The moral right of the author has been asserted

A CIP catalogue record for this book
is available from the British Library

ISBN 978-1-906598-24-2

Series design by Susan Buchanan
Typeset in Sabon by MacGuru Ltd
Printed in Dubai by Oriental Press

CONDITIONS OF SALE
All rights reserved. No part of this publication may be reproduced,
stored in a retrieval system, or transmitted in any form or by any means,
electronic, mechanical, photocopying, recording or otherwise, without
the prior permission of the publisher.

This book is sold subject to the condition that it shall not, by way of
trade or otherwise, be lent, re-sold, hired out or otherwise circulated
without the publisher's prior consent in any form of binding or cover
other than that in which it is published and without a similar condition
including this condition being imposed on the subsequent purchaser.

Contents

Preface

When a continental war broke out in Europe in August 1914, the conflict felt remote to many ordinary South Americans. But four men from the region had good reason to pay close attention to the start of hostilities. The Ecuadorian diplomat Enrique Dorn y de Alsua was not far from the scene of the fighting. The elegant, wealthy and immaculately groomed Dorn was his country's representative in France, and had lived in Paris for many years. Through his wealth of connections among the upper echelons of society the diplomat was able to give his government in Quito a clear picture of events in Europe. Francisco García Calderón was also a Paris-based diplomat, representing Peru. García Calderón was in many ways the antithesis of the sociable Dorn. An intellectual, journalist and author, the Peruvian had already written a number of influential books, one of which carried a foreword by the French Prime Minister Raymond Poincaré. García Calderón was prone to bouts of depression, and the forthcoming conflict would lead to a personal tragedy that would hit him hard.

Far away across the Atlantic Ocean, Juan Antonio Buero was also eyeing the war in Europe with unusual interest. A precociously talented young journalist, public speaker and diplomat, in 1914 the Uruguayan was rising in the ranks of his country's politicians and was already an MP. Buero, an accomplished international lawyer, also had a personal reason for his interest in the fate of Western Europe and Paris in particular; 26 years earlier he had been born there.

The fourth South American paying close attention to events across the other side of the world was the Bolivian Ismael Montes Gamboa. Like García Calderón and Dorn, Montes had once been his country's man in France. Now, however, the stocky, energetic Montes was back in La Paz having started the second of his two terms as President of Bolivia. A shrewd politician and diplomat, he understood the potentially damaging impact that the war could have on world trade – and on a country such as Bolivia that was largely dependent on exports.

The four men were very different characters. Dorn was elegant and at ease in upper class society; García Calderon a brooding, sometimes intense, often brilliant intellectual. For his part, Montes was a battle-scarred veteran of both war and Bolivian civil conflict, a wealthy landowner who wanted his country to get rich too, through free trade; finally, the ebullient Buero was a dazzling speaker and talented diplomat and journalist. Possessed of a restless intellect, he could never quite settle down to write the books he probably ought to have produced. In four-and-a-half years, however, all four men would be united around a table in Paris. Here, as representatives of their respective nations, they would take part in the momentous Peace Conference that would help to shape the modern world.

Dr Juan Antonio Buero of Uruguay and his wife, Alda Brum, together with John Barrett, the Director of the Pan American Union.

I

The Lives and the Land

1
Beginnings 1800–1900

For many if not most South Americans, the outbreak of war in Europe in August 1914 made little if any immediate difference to their lives. As news came through of the faraway conflict, it would have been hard to imagine that within a few short years delegates from four Spanish-speaking South American countries – Bolivia, Ecuador, Peru and Uruguay – would be taking part in the historic Peace Conference that followed it. Yet when one considers their history and geography, their participation at Paris becomes far more understandable.

For one thing, and despite their diverse racial mixture – at least in the case of Peru, Bolivia and Ecuador – these were countries whose development as modern nations owed much to Europe and European thought. Their very independence came as a direct result of events in the old continent, and in some cases with the help of the direct intervention of European countries and citizens. The leaders of these new states – who ran them with little reference to the masses until well into the 20th century – were inspired almost entirely by European ideas in general and French thought in particular; when in search of theories of political science and philosophy, it was to European and French writers and thinkers that most South Americans turned. This led many among the elites to take sides in the European war, intellectually if not militarily. By the early 20th century these countries had also begun to look northwards, towards the main regional political and economic power, the United States of America. The actions of the United States during the First World War and its later involvement in the subsequent Peace Conference were thus bound to have a major impact on the choices made by South American republics when it came to their own involvement in the conflict.

Equally important was the strategic importance of Latin America to both sides in the First World War. The region was a rich source of foodstuffs and raw materials, from cereals and meat, to tin and nitrates. It was also sandwiched between two vital shipping routes, one through the Panama Canal, the other round Cape Horn, and had become a battleground for trade between German, Britain and the US. When looked at in this light the question becomes less why South American countries became involved in the Paris Peace Conference and the Treaty of Versailles, and more why these particular ones – and not others. The answer to this question lies partly in the history but also in the geography of these countries; in South America, geography has had a huge impact on history and politics and continues to do so.

In racial, historic and geographic terms Peru, Bolivia, Ecuador and Uruguay fall into two 'groups'. One contains Peru, Bolivia and Ecuador, which are sometimes referred to as the Andean Republics for the obvious reason that the Andes mountain range dominates much of their topography; two of them also have long Pacific coastlines. Uruguay is altogether different. This low-lying country is on the other side of South

America and looks out on the waters of the South Atlantic Ocean. The story of Uruguay, up to and including the First World War, was often markedly dissimilar from those of the Andean Republics.

The soaring peaks of the Andes have provided the back-drop for much of the history of Ecuador, Bolivia and Peru. The capital cities of Ecuador – Quito – and Bolivia – La Paz – are both situated at high altitude. And in the case of the latter country many of its inhabitants – both pre- and post-conquest by the Spanish – have built their homes on the high Altiplano, the extraordinary plateau that lies between two ranges of the Andes and where Lake Titicaca is to be found. But mountains are not the only distinctive geographi-cal feature of the Andean Republics.

In Ecuador, for example, half of the country is made up of the Amazon rainforest, a thinly populated area that played little part in the political and economic development of the country until the 20th century. On the other side of the Andes is the coastal region of the country – *la costa* – a steamy, hot, mostly fertile area that often feels like another country from the sloping land and cooler climes of the *sierra*. Tradition-ally the people on the coast, including around the main port Guayaquil, have been regarded as more entrepreneurial, open and liberal, while those in the mountains – around Quito where political power generally resided – are seen as more conservative. Indeed, for much of the 19th century it was hard to regard Ecuador as a functioning, unified country, and even to this day the rivalries between *los costeños* and the *serranos* are deep and sometimes bitter.

In Peru, too, differences of geography have had a huge impact on the country's development. Unlike those of its Andean neighbours, Peru's capital and most important city,

Lima, is on the coast. This has led the city's inhabitants and its rulers to look outwards towards the sea or north or south along the coast rather than focusing on the mountainous interior to the east. Many of the upper classes of Lima in the late 19th and early 20th century would have been more familiar with European and North American cities than they would have been with Peru's Andean towns and cities. Beyond those famous mountains – well-known today for their astonishing Incan heritage – lie what are called the *montaña*, the forested hills that lead into the jungle region and much of which was remote and inaccessible at the end of the 19th century. Much of Peru's mostly dry coastline, meanwhile, was found to be rich in both nitrates and *guano* – the nitrate and phosphate-rich remains of bird droppings that had been used as a fertiliser by the Incas – and which were to bring both prosperity and misfortune in late 19th century Peru.

Even in Bolivia, where much of its history and population has been dominated by the 500-mile-long Altiplano, other physical features in the landscape have played their part. During the 19th century the country had a small but strategically important coastline, one that was also rich in nitrates. Bolivia lost this in a disastrous war with Chile that broke out in 1879, a loss that was to have a major impact on Bolivia's later foreign policy – including at the Paris Peace Conference. To the east of the mountains are deep, plunging fertile valleys followed by flat plains that extend to the Amazon in one direction and to the south-east through dry, scrub forest terrain known as the Chaco. It was over this isolated, and in places, forbidding, area that Bolivia was to fight another disastrous war, this time in the first half of the 20th century.

The landscape of Uruguay could scarcely be more different from the three Andean countries. Its highest hills do not even reach 1,700 feet and the entire country falls within the temperate climate zone; it typically has cool, damp but not very cold winters, warm to hot summers and mild autumns. Uruguay is also a land dominated by water, with the River Uruguay forming its frontier with neighbouring Argentina, the wide waters of the Río de la Plata or River Plate to the south and the Atlantic Ocean itself to the east. Unlike the Andean Republics, transport and communications are not a problem across this small, low-lying country. Its beaches have also made Uruguay something of a playground for residents from neighbouring countries, notably the resort of Punta del Este, 90 miles to the east of the capital city, Montevideo.

Another key difference between Uruguay and the other three Spanish-speaking South American countries invited to Paris can be seen in its racial make-up, an issue that is always close to the surface when discussing the political and social history of the region. During the period between the early 16th century when Europeans first landed in what is now Uruguay, until its creation as a country in the early 19th century, the indigenous Charrúa people were largely wiped out or integrated with the settlers. Little now is known of these people and Uruguay's population is predominantly white and European in origin – specifically Spanish and Italian.

> 'The history of the southern peoples is full of revolutions, rich with dreams of an unattainable perfection.'
>
> FRANCISCO GARCÍA CALDERÓN

The contrast with the Andean Republics, where the populations are overwhelmingly Indian or mixed race – *mestizo* – could hardly be greater. In the last official count that used racial categories, the 1940 census in Peru reported that some 46 per cent of the population was Indian. This figure was

NATIVE AMERICANS IN BOLIVIA, ECUADOR, PERU AND URUGUAY
Ethnicity has and continues to play a key role in Latin American politics and society, and nowhere more so in the Andean Republics of Bolivia, Ecuador and Peru where sizeable proportions of the populations are native Indians. These countries are made up of a minority of pure white descendants from Spanish settlers, plus Amerindians and mixed-race *mestizos* as they are usually known in Spanish. When the Spanish arrived in what is now Bolivia in the 16th century they found the Inca kingdom dominating the area. However, the Incas had themselves only recently arrived in the area, and the Altiplano of high plains had previously been inhabited by the Aymara people, who continued to live there during Inca times. To this day many Bolivians are of Aymaran descent and speak Aymara. The Quechua-speaking descendants of the Incas make up another significant part of the population; in all, around 55 per cent of the inhabitants are Amerindians. The capital of the Inca empire was Cusco in modern-day Peru, and that country still has many Quechua speakers as well as those who speak Aymara. The Inca empire spread as far north as Ecuador but here too, as in the other Andean Republics, there are also the descendants of other indigenous peoples. The independence of these nations at the start of the 19th century made little difference to the Indians, other than losing the official protected status they had enjoyed under Spanish colonial laws. In theory, the aim of governments was to bring native people into the emerging capitalist economies and societies that were developing; in practice, many lived in parallel universes from the Westernised system. There was also an inherent conflict between large landowners who wanted to expand their holdings and Indian *comunidades*, which were often the victims of these land-grabs. By contrast, in Uruguay the native Charrúa had essentially vanished by the time of independence, and most Uruguayans are of Spanish or Italian origin.

probably an underestimate. Today the figure is thought to be around 45 per cent, with *mestizos* making up around 37 per cent. The pure white population – who have for much of Peru's history dominated political power – has usually been around 15 per cent. Whites make up a similar percentage of the population in Ecuador, where the dominant racial group are the mixed-race *mestizos*, with Amerindians making up about a quarter of the population. The coastal region in and around Esmeraldas also has a significant African-Ecuadorian population. No one is quite sure how they came to arrive in South America but it is thought that they may be the descendants of slaves from a ship that was either shipwrecked or commandeered. In Bolivia it is the Amerindians who make up more than 50 per cent of the population, split between the Quechua and Aymara peoples with whites once again making up just around 15 per cent of the population.

The racial make-up of the Andean Republics matters, not least because it has caused a great deal of soul-searching and discussion about identity in those nations. Until the First World War there was a widespread feeling among much of these countries' elites and intelligentsia that their blend of Latin (Spanish) and Indian blood boded ill for their futures. This 'racial pessimism' was in keeping with racial theories much in vogue in Europe at the time. The distinguished writer and intellectual Francisco García Calderón, who was to become one of Peru's delegates at the Paris Peace Conference, for a time shared this gloomy view about South America's heritage and future, because of both its Latin and Indian roots. On the eve of the war García Calderón wrote that race was the *key to the incurable disorder that divides [Latin] America*. The Peruvian was acutely aware of what he then saw as key differences between the Anglo-Saxons who dominated the United States to the north and those of Latin heritage who held sway in Latin America. *Essential points of difference separate the two Americas … in their origin, as in their race, we find fundamental antagonism; the evolution of the North is slow and obedient to the lessons of time, to the influences of custom; the history of the southern peoples is full of revolutions, rich with dreams of an unattainable perfection*. However, in the coming years he came to adopt a more positive view of Latin America and Peru and their racial mix. For him the future lay in the *brilliant and lazy* Creole or white Latin American of European (usually Spanish or Portuguese) descent, and García Calderón came to be described as a 'leading apostle of Americanism and of solidarity among the Latin races'.[1]

Though Uruguay's racial make-up and past was very different from that of the Andean Republics, it did share one important factor with at least two of them. For Uruguay, like Bolivia and Ecuador, and arguably even Peru too, was a buffer zone between other, more powerful neighbours. The complex picture of South American history and politics often resembles a Rubik's Cube; try to solve one problem in one area and it will likely have an impact – often negative – in another. Managing the complicated series of shifting alliances between neighbours and near-neighbours was an essential tactic for smaller South American nations trying to protect themselves against bigger, more powerful countries such as Argentina, Chile and Brazil. Sometimes this manoeuvring involved trying to enlist the support of the United States, in the hope that it could provide protection. This calculated need to attract the attention of Washington was to play its part in the decision of these four countries to side with the Allies and break off relations with Germany during the First World War.[2]

Uruguay's status as a buffer zone can be seen clearly from a glance at a map of the region. Its two neighbours are the biggest powers in South America – Argentina and Brazil – and this basic geo-political reality has always influenced Uruguayan diplomacy. Indeed, the country was specifically created *as* a buffer zone between the rival Spanish-speaking Argentineans and the Portuguese-speaking Brazilians.

The first Europeans to set foot in what was to become Uruguay were members of an expedition led by Juan Díaz de Solís, who landed east of what is now the capital city Montevideo in 1516. He had been searching for a way of sailing from the Atlantic to the Pacific and sailed up the wide Río de la Plata thinking that was a potential route. Legend has it that Solís and all his landing party – save for a cabin boy – were killed and eaten by the native Charrúa Indians. There are now doubts about the accuracy of all of the story – Solís may have been killed by the Guaraní Indians – but there is little doubt he met his end in what is now Uruguay. Over the next decades and centuries this area did not attract as much attention from Spanish explorers and settlers as other parts of South America such as Peru; for one thing there were no alluring stories of gold and silver.

At the start of the 17th century the first locally born governor of Río de la Plata – what is now Argentina – Hernando Arias, arranged for 100 cattle and 100 horses to be sent to this vast area of grasslands across the water. Over the ensuing decades these animals bred to such an extent that by the third decade of the 18th century there were an estimated 25 million cattle in the region. These animals became a sought-after prize for the Spanish from Buenos Aires, and gauchos and merchants began to move into the area. Another incentive for the Spanish to control the territory was the arrival of the Portuguese on the opposite side of the Río de la Plata from Buenos Aires. This was the start of fierce rivalry between the Spanish and Portuguese over this important but still sparsely-populated buffer zone. At the time the land was known as the Banda Oriental del Río Uruguay – the east bank of the River Uruguay.

At the beginning of the 19th century the Banda became a

place of conflict between not just the Spanish and the Portuguese, but involving, too, pro-Imperial Spanish and local-born Spanish or Creoles, and also the British. In 1807 a British expedition – without formal sanction from London – occupied Montevideo after failing to take the better-defended Buenos Aires. This force left after just seven months after failing once again to defeat the Spanish garrison in Buenos Aires. But the following year European politics intervened in the history of the country when Napoleon deposed the Spanish monarchy and installed his own ruler in Spain. This unleashed the process that was, over the course of the next two decades, to lead to the independence of the South American colonies from Spanish rule. The American and French revolutions were also still fresh in people's minds, and the instability in Spain led to attempts by Creoles – local-born whites of Spanish origin – to proclaim independence. At the time the Banda had little apparent prospect of becoming an independent state. The people of Buenos Aires regarded the land as theirs, while the Portuguese in Brazil also coveted the area and its strategically-important ports. Britain, however, which had strong commercial interests in the region, wanted neither Buenos Aires nor Brazil to get their hands on the territory. At the same time a sense of Banda national identity – that saw loyalty neither to Buenos Aires nor Brazil – was emerging, articulated by a local gaucho called José Gervasio Artigas.

Artigas and a small but hardy band of horsemen fought in turn against the Spanish, the people of Buenos Aires and the Portuguese. By 1820 his mission appeared to have ended in failure, as he was unable to prevent the Banda being annexed by Brazil and re-named Cisplatine Province. However, Artigas' heroics had forged a local identity, and in 1825 another patriot called Juan Antonio Lavalleja led a band

THE WARS OF INDEPENDENCE FROM SPAIN 1808–26
The first attempt at independence was in La Paz in Upper Peru – now Bolivia. The Spanish authorities quickly restored order in many areas and the wars of independence ensued between forces from Spain on one side and local Creole elites and *mestizos* (people of mixed race) on the other. The Spanish American Creoles – who had economic reasons for wanting independence – were helped by a number of mercenaries from Europe, mostly English, Scots and Irish. The great hero of independence was Simón Bolívar, born in Caracas in 1783, who later gave his name to the new country of Bolivia. Bolívar was part-visionary, part-soldier, and his twin aims were to liberate South American from Spanish rule and to create a federation of states. In the former he, with the help of a number of fine generals such as José de San Martin from what is now Argentina, was ultimately successful by 1826. In the latter, however, he failed absolutely; even his plan to unite Venezuela, Colombia and Ecuador into one state called Gran Colombia fell apart. Instead, independent republics developed, broadly based upon the boundaries of the former Spanish colonial administrative area. The fact that in some cases these boundaries were ill-defined and certainly ill-suited to sovereign nations was to be the cause of considerable conflict between the independent republics in the coming decades.

of 33 fighters – a group that has since been immortalised in Uruguayan history – across the Río Plata from the Argentine side to liberate the Banda. With help from Argentina – which assumed it would be able to incorporate the Banda as one of its own provinces – and receiving popular support, the patriots led a major revolt against Brazilian rule in Montevideo. The British, however, were alarmed that their vital trade interests would be threatened should either Brazil or Argentina seize definitive control over the province, and London intervened to broker an agreement between those two countries. In 1828 it was finally agreed that the former Banda – with a population of little more than 60,000 – would become a fully-fledged republic of its own, to be called the República Oriental del Uruguay.

Uruguay's survival as a separate state, however, was still far from certain. Local politics had already split into two main factions. One was led by a member of the 'Thirty-Three', Manuel Oribe, whose supporters wore white. Broadly speaking these 'Blancos', as they became called, were seen as conservative and rural-based. The other group was led by Oribe's predecessor as president, José Fructuoso Rivera, whose supporters wore red. The 'Colorados', as they became known, were generally seen as more liberal and progressive. These two factions were to dominate Uruguayan politics for many decades to come, during which time the distinctions between the parties and what they stood for were not always clear. More immediately, however, the two factions became involved in a bitter battle for the fate of Uruguay itself, when Fructuoso Rivera fell out with Argentine dictator and strong-man Manuel Rosas, and found himself under attack from a combined force of Blanco supporters and Argentinean troops. From 1843 until 1851 – when Rosas himself faced internal revolt – the city of Montevideo stood firm against attack. It was a siege that inspired not just the people of Uruguay but international public opinion too. The French writer Alexandre Dumas was moved to write a book in which he loftily described Montevideo as the 'New Troy', while the future hero of Italian reunification, Giuseppe Garibaldi, led a group of fighters on the city's behalf. This was the first occasion on which they donned their soon-to-be famous red shirts.

Though the date of the lifting of the siege is now celebrated in Uruguay, the years that followed it were far from joyful. A grim pattern set in, during which the Colorados dominated power, with the Blancos opposing them, sometimes violently. One Uruguayan president needed Brazilian support to stay in power. In return he committed the country to fighting alongside Brazil and Argentina in a bloody war against Paraguay from 1865 to 1870. Ten years after that war ended, another Uruguayan president quit office apparently claiming that the country – or rather its people – were ungovernable. The stark figures tend to support his claim. Out of 25 governments formed between 1830 and 1903, only three were free of serious violence and disturbance, nine were forced out of office and two cut short by assassination. Yet just two decades into the 20th century this divided, factional country was being held up as a model of social reform and progress, and one whose role on the world stage was praised. [3]

It was late in this unsettling period in Uruguayan history – 1888 – that Juan Antonio Buero was born, the man who would be his country's delegate at the 1919 Peace Conference. Buero, however, was born not in his native country but in Paris, a fact that would make his return to the French capital to take part in the Conference especially poignant. The son of Enrique Buero and Maria Thevenet – who was descended from a French family – Buero was educated in France and later Brazil and Argentina before finally taking a law degree at Montevideo University. This cosmopolitan background helped equip the young man for his future career as an international lawyer, diplomat and politician; noted for his intelligence and sharp mind, he spoke five languages – Spanish, French, German, Portuguese and English – and was a gifted orator at a time when the art of public speaking was an important accomplishment. His experience would also make him an obvious choice to represent his country at Paris.

Far away, across South America's mighty rivers and mountains, Ecuador had been following a very different, if equally turbulent, course to that of Uruguay. The area that was to become Ecuador lay on the edge of the Spanish empire. The city of Quito and territory roughly equating to modern-day Ecuador was made the seat of a high court or *audencia*, giving the area some degree of autonomy, though it was attached to the more important and wealthier Viceroyalty of Peru to the south. In 1739 the Spanish reassigned Quito to the new Viceroyalty of New Granada, made up of what is today Colombia, Panama and Venezuela as well as Ecuador. Meanwhile the area's main port Guayaquil, a strategically-important city that depended largely on the cacao trade, had developed an identity different to and independent from the distant Andean city of Quito.

When the Spanish-American wars of independence began, Guayaquil's merchants hoped to carve out a status as an independent city-state. Another less welcome option was to become part of an independent Peru – as one of the heroes of South American independence, José de San Martín, wanted. There was certainly little desire to be subordinated to Quito. However, the great hero of Spanish-American independence, Simón Bolívar, had other ideas. His aim was to create a new state of Gran Colombia – including Colombia, Panama and Venezuela as well as Quito – and for him the Pacific port of Guayaquil was a vital element of that plan. San Martín and Bolívar met in Guayaquil in July 1822 to discuss the city's fate and the outcome was clear; it became part of Gran Colombia.

Bolívar's great dream only lasted until 1830, when Gran Colombia fell apart under pressure from Venezuela as old tensions and jealousies from Spanish colonial times reappeared to influence this new era of independence. The citizens of Quito and Guayaquil were equally disgruntled. Despite their differences, these cities and the surrounding populations were united in resenting the rule of Bogotá, capital of the new state. They now feared they had simply swapped one form of colonial dictatorship for another. So as Gran Colombia disintegrated, the people of the old Quito *audiencia* declared independence and on 13 May 1830 the new country of Ecuador was born. However, as with Uruguay, Ecuador's independence hardly heralded the start of a golden era. The squabbles between the powerful merchants of Guayaquil and the political power-brokers of Quito meant that Ecuador barely functioned as a state in those early decades. The means of communication between the two cities were as poor as their relationship, while in and around the port itself the danger of yellow fever made it a perilous place for foreigners to visit. The country was also saddled with a massive debt owed by Gran Colombia to Britain for that country's help in supporting its independence. The rest of the century would witness a plethora of new governments and a succession of new constitutions but precious little political stability.

The most influential figure in the early days of the newly-independent country was Juan José Flores, a Venezuelan soldier who had married into the upper echelons of Quito society, and who became the country's first president. An ambitious man, he seemed to have a limitless thirst for power, and when not ruling the country he was involved in plots to invade it and seize back control. The conservative Flores' biggest rival was a liberal named Vicente Rocafuerte, and these two men represented the two political tendencies that would dominate Ecuadorian politics for many years. The conservatives were generally pro-Church and tended to find most of their support in Quito, while support for the anti-clerical liberals was usually to be found among the merchants of Guayaquil. The bitter rivalry between these factions and individual caudillos or military leaders threatened to bring the country to its knees. In 1859 – known among the country's historians as the 'Terrible Year' – the towns of Cuenca and Loja declared their independence, there were moves to link Guayaquil to Peru, a Peruvian army threatened to carve up the country and the emerging new conservative leader Gabriel García Moreno was secretly discussing the possibility of the country becoming a French protectorate – and offering parts of the Amazon basin and the Galapágos Islands in return.

Moreno's plans were quickly abandoned once they became public. But even without French help the pro-clerical leader was able to stabilise the country and usher in a new era of relative calm and limited economic progress, even if revolts and rebellions remained part of the political fabric of the country. By August 1875 Moreno's political stock had fallen, and the unfortunate politician was hacked to death with a machete outside the presidential palace in Quito. This provoked yet more conflict between Church and liberals, between the merchants of Guayaquil and the conservative landowners of the *sierra*. To give just one more gruesome example of events in this period, the Archbishop of Quito died on Good Friday, 1877, after drinking from a poisoned chalice as he presided over a service.

For much of the rest of the 19th century the country was largely dominated by the conservatives. And with the cacao industry doing well and the sugar industry emerging, the country made some economic progress amid relative political calm, even if political power still lay in the hands of just a small section of society. But the liberal-conservative divide had not gone away. In 1895 yet another civil war saw the Liberals finally triumph in the person of the veteran José Eloy Alfaro Delgado, who was strongly anti-clerical, was known as *el Viejo Luchador* or the 'Old Fighter' because of his dogged attempts to achieve power over the years. Now at the age of

53 he had finally attained it and began an era of Liberal rule in Ecuador.

By the time Alfaro came to power, the country's future delegate at the Peace Conference was already out of the country – in Paris. Enrique Dorn y de Alsua, who was born in 1845, and whose family had links with Vicente Rocafuerte, was working at his country's diplomatic mission in France. José Flores's son Antonio Flores Jijón had become Ecuadorian Minister in France in 1861 and when later in 1882 he became president, he was keen to ensure his country's representation in France was maintained. In particular, Flores Jijón wanted Ecuador to be represented at the Paris Universal Exhibition, which coincided with the centenary of the French Revolution – a landmark event for independent Spanish-American republics. Ecuadorian participation was bankrolled by wealthy businessmen from the country's coastal area and the government set up an Official Commission in Paris to oversee the setting-up of its pavilion. This commission's secretary was Enrique Dorn y de Alsua. As was the case with Buero, Dorn's experience of France, fluent French and network of contacts were to make this wealthy, dapper man a good choice to represent his country in the French capital 20 years later.

Unlike Ecuador, the Viceroyalty of Peru had been at the heart of Spanish colonial activity in South America where the lure of Inca gold and then the country's productive mines proved a major attraction. It has been estimated that during the period of colonial rule – from the early 16th century to the early 19th century – well over two billion pesos of bullion was taken from the country's mines.[4] This figure includes Upper Peru (also known as Charcas) as well as Peru itself – the former later became Bolivia. Little wonder, then that the City of Kings, better known as Lima, attracted some of the most ambitious and well-connected Spanish aristocrats who came to the New World and that it developed all the trappings of a major city. Its University of San Marcos, for example, was founded in 1551. It was also the royalist and conservative stronghold of the Spanish South American Empire, and a place where a white population of just 13 per cent dominated the rest of the people. It was perhaps symbolic, then, that the man who liberated Lima from the Spanish was an outsider, José de San Martín, who was born in the Río de la Plata viceroyalty. It was he who entered the city and declared independence on 28 July 1821. The Spanish royalists were not yet completely beaten, however, and they briefly reoccupied the city in 1823 and continued the struggle in the interior of the country until Bolívar and his generals were able to claim final victory on 9 December 1824 after the Battle of Ayacucho. As for the city's wealthy elites, they were split. Some saw independence as a way of continuing with the same conservative way of government as before, except without Spain. Others pushed for (limited) liberal reforms. One thing was certain, however; the majority Indian population were to have little or no say in the governing of the country even though it was independent of Spain for the first time in 300 years. As elsewhere in South America, this was essentially an upper middle-class/elite revolution.

The early years of Peruvian independence were perhaps inevitably dominated by struggles between military strongmen or *caudillos*. Economically, too, the new country suffered problems, not least because it had been ravaged by war – including the key port city of Callao – and now faced competition from ports on the east coast of South America whose use had previously been restricted by the Spanish. There were also doubts, too, about the very boundaries of

Peru, a common theme among South American republics in the 19th century. On 6 August 1825, Upper Peru separated from Peru to become the independent country of Bolivia, despite misgivings from Bolívar himself. Yet in the 1830s the Bolivian leader Andrés Santa Cruz proposed reuniting the two countries into a confederation divided into three semi-autonomous provinces – North Peru, South Peru and Bolivia. He eventually succeeded in achieving this dream in 1836, and for three years this shaky confederation survived. It was swept away in 1839, partly because of opposition within Peru but above all because of opposition from Argentina and especially Chile, whose troops defeated those of Santa Cruz at the critical Battle of Yungay. Both Chile and Argentina feared that the new confederation would affect the balance of power in the region.

The following couple of decades in Peru were what is sometimes known as the 'Guano Age'. The accumulation of this valuable fertiliser plus the discovery of nitrate deposits on the arid Peruvian coastline were to provide a major source of wealth for the Peruvian government – and foreign firms. The first consignment of Peru's guano arrived in Liverpool in 1841. Yet the great wealth the guano brought also had its downsides. In particular the Peruvian government became dependent on guano at the expense of developing other, more sustainable parts of its economy. The dominant political figure at this time was Ramón Castilla, a distinguished military officer who harboured dreams of a more united South America as a counterbalance to the growing power of the United States. Twice president of Peru, Castilla's rule brought a degree of stability to the country and the wealth provided by the guano trade even allowed him to promote some social legislation – for example the freeing of the country's black slaves. Castilla also oversaw the development of a properly-paid civil service and the start of public works, such as the building of roads, bridges, gaslights and sanitation infrastructure in Lima. It was also under him that Latin America's first railway was built, running from Lima to Callao on the coast, opening in 1851.

Though it lasted for many decades, the Guano Age proved to be a wasted opportunity for Peru. One writer noted that the wealth it produced had led to the 'corruption and laziness of the majority of the citizens' and had 'actually discouraged people from seeking riches in agriculture and manufacturing'.[5] Later in the century the nitrate boom moved further down the coast, offering the chances for more wealth but eventually leading to friction between Peru and Bolivia and Chile. Ultimately this led to the War of the Pacific (1879–83).

The war was a disaster for Peru. It led to losses of territory and money, disrupted business and humiliated the country and its politicians. Just about the only people to emerge with any credit were those sections of the military perceived to have fought with bravery against the superior might of the Chileans. Appropriately enough, therefore, it was a soldier, General Andrés Cáceres, who seized control of the

WAR OF THE PACIFIC 1879–83
The War of the Pacific was fought between Chile on one side and Peru and Bolivia on the other. The immediate stated cause of the war was Chile's anger at the treatment of its nationals working in the lucrative nitrates industry in Bolivia's coastal area. War between the two countries provoked Peru to join in on Bolivia's side. Chile won a decisive military victory and seized land from Peru and also all of Bolivia's coastline. The outcome confirmed Chile as a major power in the region and also fomented continuing discontent in Peru and Bolivia over their loss of territory, which they both sought to raise at the Paris Peace Conference. In particular Chile seized the Peruvian provinces of Tacna and Arica, areas that would feature in later disputes and negotiations involving Chile and Peru and also Bolivia, which had long coveted the port of Arica itself and had now lost its entire coastline.

government and who effectively ran Peru from 1885 to 1895, first as president and then as the power behind his own hand-picked successor. The most notable event during his time in power was the signing of the so-called Grace Contract. Peru, in common with some other South American countries, was enormously in debt to bondholders, who in this case were based in London. A representative of these disgruntled bond-holders, Michael A Grace, came to Lima to broker a deal over those debts, which at face value were close to £50 million. The controversial result was that the foreign bondholders gained control of the country's railways for 66 years, had the rights to up to three million tons of guano a year that was not needed for domestic use, and were to receive an annual payment of £80,000. In return the bondholders agreed to advance further loans of up to £6 million. Though this was a deal that Peru probably had little choice but to accept, the Grace Contract became for nationalists a shameful symbol of the role that foreign powers and investors played in Peruvian affairs.

Cáceres' attempts to return as president provoked a bloody revolt, and there was fierce fighting on the streets of Lima where up to 3,000 people were killed in March 1895. The man to emerge as the country's new leader and president was Nicolás de Pièrola, who had created his own Democrat Party and was influenced by neo-positivist thought, a pre-vailing political philosophy in many parts of Latin America at the time. He placed emphasis on reform of institutions and the financial system, on education and on modernising the country. This was a time of change in Peruvian society and ideas. A new generation of intellectuals who attended San Marcos University were heavily influenced by the Uru-guayan writer José Enrique Rodo's book *Ariel*, published in 1900, and were often described as the '1900s Generation' or alternatively 'Arielists'. A major theme of this group was the importance of spiritual and cultural values of their country over simple materialism.

One of this generation was Francisco García Calderón. A hallmark of the 1900s Generation was that they were marked – scarred even – by Peru's humiliation in the war with Chile and the need to modernise their country. In García Calderón's case his experience of the war was a very personal one. His father – also called Francisco García Calderón – was a distinguished lawyer who had briefly been president of Peru during the War of the Pacific in 1881. Francisco junior was himself born two years later in Valparaiso, where the Chilean authorities were holding his father a prisoner. A year later the family was allowed to leave Chile and they headed for Europe; Francisco's younger brother Ventura was born in Paris in 1886. It was not until later that year that the family returned to Peru for the first time since Francisco's birth. He was destined to spend much of the rest of his life away, too, from the country. However, his school years were spent in Lima, studying at the prestigious new college at Recoleta, founded in 1885.

Given their shared history, the late colonial history and independence of Bolivia obviously had much in common with that of Peru. As already mentioned, Bolivia was created out of what had been known in colonial times as Upper Peru, a source of much of the country's mineral wealth. It took its name in honour of Bolívar, despite the great Liberator's own misgivings about the creation of the country. Some historians have claimed that there was no real logic to having an independent Bolivia, based on its past and its identity. The key reason for its creation, so this argument goes, was to stop Peru and Argentina, countries with a history and interest in the wealth of Bolivia, quarrelling over the area.

Río de la Plata (later Argentina) had been given control over Upper Peru in 1776. Bolivians, however, insist that there was a sense of national identity both before and during the wars of independence, and certainly before it became an independent state in 1825. Nonetheless, Bolivia was created in a somewhat precarious geo-political situation, with powerful Argentina to the south, ambitious Chile to the south-west and Peru to the north, and possessed a relatively small strip of territory on the Pacific coast.

The first ruler of Bolivia was Antonio José de Sucre, the gifted military officer who had liberated the area. But it was Andrés Santa Cruz, mentioned above, and whose mother was said to have been descended from Incan nobility, who was to have a big influence in the early years of the new republic. Before his ill-fated attempt to create a confederation with Peru, which ended in exile, Santa Cruz managed to create a remarkably stable economy and country during a decade in power. He was succeeded eventually by José Ballivián, another strongman or caudillo who succeeded in creating relative stability in Bolivia until 1847. His biggest weakness was his passion for women – other men's women. On one occasion he had to flee for his life over the rooftops from a jealous husband. This was the man who would succeed him as president, Manuel Isidoro Belzu. It was said of Ballivián that he had 'placed in danger the honour of all the married women of Bolivia'.[6]

The following decades in Bolivia proved to be turbulent ones politically, even though by the 1860s and the 1870s the country's wealth had started to grow. Partly this prosperity was due to improved technology in the mining of silver in the Altiplano, but also because of the discovery of nitrates on the Bolivian coastal strip. This industry was dominated by Chilean and British interests, and for many years Bolivian governments were content to sit back and enjoy the income that came in from selling concessions. Despite intermittent protests they did little to discourage Chilean encroachment on their territory and governments – for example the dictatorship of General Mariano Melgarejo from 1864 to 1870 – and were later accused of selling the country to foreign interests. Then, as with Peru, the Bolivian economy suffered when depression hit the world economy. Worse was to come when in 1878 the hard-pressed Bolivian government demanded more tax receipts from the nitrates produced by Anglo-Chilean interests. The ensuing War of the Pacific was a conflict that Chile had apparently been anticipating, even wanting, for some time. The outcome for Bolivia was every bit as bad as it was for Peru. Worst of all, the loss of its coastal territory left Bolivia land-locked, later forcing the country to look eastwards towards the Atlantic for a coastal outlet. The issue of Bolivia's lost Pacific coast was one that would dog the country for many decades to come, before, during and after the Paris Peace Conference.

'A country in itself has nothing.'
ISMAEL MONTES

The period after the war and up to 1899 was dominated by the Conservative Party and by the involvement of the country's powerful silver mine owners in politics. At the same time the interests of the majority population – in 1900 some 51 per cent of the population was indigenous – were largely ignored. As had sometimes occurred under colonial rule, this occasionally provoked violent revolts. In 1899 the Liberals staged a revolt in Bolivia, with its leader José Manuel Pando winning Indian support for his actions when he promised to address their grievances. In power, the Liberals once more overlooked the Indian grievances, provoking a massive and bloody uprising by indigenous groups.

The Liberals, however, were able to hold on to power. And one of their principal figures in the coming years was Ismael Montes Gamboa, future president and the country's delegate at Paris in 1919. Born in 1861 into a wealthy landowning family, Montes had fought in the War of the Pacific before training as a lawyer. A stocky, hardworking and shrewd politician, Montes was to prove himself a whole-hearted supporter of economic liberalism. *A country in itself has nothing*, he wrote. *Its wealth is nothing more than the sum of private wealth. Therefore it is scientifically necessary to stimulate the growth of the latter so that it will contribute with the greatest effectiveness to the national prosperity.*[7] There was little doubt that wealth accumulation was something that a lucky few achieved during the early years of the 20th century as both Bolivia and other parts of South America experienced an age of economic liberalism.

2

On the Eve of War 1900–14

The start of the 20th century marked the beginning of a new era in the Andean Republics. This was, in theory at least, a time when liberalism and free trade were at their peak in Bolivia, Ecuador and to a lesser extent Peru. It would be wrong, though, to describe this as a golden period for the three countries, not least because the bulk of the population, including the indigenous peoples, saw little or nothing of this prosperity. But thanks to the mineral earnings and burgeoning agriculture of these countries, it was a time when their elites shared considerable wealth and when the infrastructure of Ecuador, Bolivia and Peru began to develop.

This period also saw a growth in trade ties between the United States and much of Latin America as the first shoots of continental co-operation – under the title of Pan-Americanism – began to emerge. The rather tentative inaugural International Conference of American States had taken place back in 1889 in Washington. The second one did not occur until 1901 – this time in Mexico – but this was followed more swiftly by a third in 1905 in Brazil and then a fourth in Argentina in 1910. None of these conferences could be considered resounding successes, nor did they resolve major problems. Indeed, some in Latin America accused Washington of effectively hijacking and controlling the gatherings. But they did at least give Latin American nations a glimpse of the potential role of pan-American co-operation, and opened continental diplomatic eyes towards the possible uses of such meetings.

For countries such as Peru, the International American Conferences were above all a chance to resolve key issues relating to its borders. Peru was surrounded on all sides by border disputes, including long-running ones with Ecuador, and issues with Colombia, Bolivia, Brazil and most of all Chile – which still held Tacna and Arica after the War of the Pacific. Under the subsequent Treaty of Ancón, there was supposed to have been plebiscites held in 1893 in both Tacna and Arica, allowing the populations to decide their own fate. Neither country could agree on how this should be done, however, and the two areas remained under Chilean control. Peru was not content to let the matter rest and tried to use the second and third American Conferences to force Chile into compulsory and binding arbitration on the issue. In the event Chile succeeded in avoiding obligatory arbitration of the dispute, despite Peruvian complaints that as time dragged on the disputed areas were gradually being 'Chileanized'. During this same period, between the start of the 20th century and the First World War, Peru was also careful to develop closer ties with the United States. Lima saw Washington as a potential ally against growing Chilean domination of the region. In turn the United States – though unwilling to take sides against Chile – was equally keen to ensure stability in an area that was becoming increasingly important for US trade. From 1900 to 1913 US exports to South America rose in value from $38 million to $146 million.

Peruvian leaders also had their own economic reasons to establish closer ties with the US. Though by the start of the First World War Britain would still be a bigger investor that the US, the latter's total investments in the country still reached $50 million. US and British cash was coming into the country to build the country's railways, modernise and fund mining and improve the infrastructure for Peru's growing agricultural exports. This was a time of rapid expansion in Peru's sugar and cotton plantations. The amount of money pouring into Peru – and out of it – during this pre-war period is shown by the fact that the number of banks in Lima rose from four to ten. Meanwhile from 1900 to the eve of war the country benefited from a positive balance of trade every year.[1]

An American traveller who went through Peru on his way back from the first Pan American Scientific Congress held in Santiago in December 1908 later wrote a fascinating account of his trip. Hiram Bingham – the man who in 1911 would rediscover the 'lost city' of Machu Picchu in Peru – emphasised the potential of Peru and Latin America for trade and also gamely tried to dispel a few myths, while at the same time perpetuating a few quaint American stereotypes about their Latin neighbours along the way: 'It is particularly important that we should realize that the political conditions of the larger republics are very much more stable than our newspaper and novel-reading public are aware of. Lynchings are unheard of ... Serious riots, such as some of our largest American cities have seen within the past generation, are no more common with them than with us. It is true that the Latin temperament finds it much more difficult to bow to the majesty of the law and to yield gracefully to governmental decrees than the more phlegmatic Teuton or Anglo-Saxon. But the revolutions and riots that Paris has witnessed during the past century have not kept us from a serious effort to increase our business with France. The occasional political riot that takes place, of no more significance than the riots caused by strikers with which we are all too familiar at home, is no reason why we should be afraid to endeavor to capture the South American market. There is not the slightest question that there is a great opportunity awaiting the American manufacturer and exporter when he is willing to grasp it with intelligent persistence and determination. South America is ready to take American goods in very large quantities as soon as we are ready to take time to give attention to her needs.'[2]

The domestic politics of Peru at this time were dominated by what is described as 'bossism'. The upper classes and business classes kept power among themselves thanks to a very limited suffrage with no secret ballot. This left those who were able to vote open to pressure from landowners and bosses. The most able of the presidents at this time was José Pardo, an accomplished lawyer who had won acclaim for the way he had fought Peru's case in boundary disputes with Ecuador and Bolivia, always key issues in Peru. He had a political pedigree, too, as his father Manuel had been a respected president who had set up the country's first true political party – the Civilistas – before being assassinated in 1878. His son was to be president twice, once before and once during the First World War. Pardo junior was praised for the way he oversaw Peru's economic mini-boom at this time, including the development of a rubber production in the country's Amazon region. He also promoted some modest social legislation to protect workers, though this took some years to come into law. They would not be enough, however, to ward off serious industrial unrest in the country in the coming years. Pardo also built up the country's navy, aware that disputes with neighbouring countries were certain to remain a constant source of tension.

A measure of the relative calm of Pardo's administration is shown by the measured way he ended his term in office. The former president left not just the presidential palace, but Peru itself, preferring to stay in Europe until 1914 to give his successor – his treasury minister Augusto B Leguía – a freer hand. However, Hiram Bingham's suggestion that Peru was no less stable than the US was not entirely true. Before Leguía's election in 1908 an opposition politician had unsuccessfully tried to stage a revolution. Beneath the apparently orderly surface, there were many sources of potential unrest in Peru at this time, despite the prosperity sections of the population were enjoying.

Though Britain and increasingly the United States were key overseas players in relation to Peru's economy and politics, Germany's influence was significant also. In 1907 German trade with the South American country was worth just over half that of Britain. There were other links too. Wireless telegraphy, essential equipment for the Peruvian navy, had been introduced to the country by a German firm Telefunken-Gesellschaft. In 1905, meanwhile, the country raised a £600,000 loan through a German bank, the German Transatlantic Bank, which established branches in Callao and Arequipa. German businesses were also investing in railway projects, and owned a number of steamship companies. The tonnage of German shipping arriving at Callao in this pre-war period was surpassed only by British vessels. Meanwhile the Peruvian upper classes, who often employed Europeans to educate their children in the culture of the Old World, had a penchant for German governesses.

The strength of German interests in Peru at this time did

not go unnoticed among other European countries. 'The entrance of German capital into the field of railway investment in South America is an evidence of a new policy, of a wider outreaching, on the part of Germans, and doubtless they will continue to push forward in various ways, besides trading, in the vast southern continent,' wrote one observer in 1911. And as a European conflict looked ever more likely, Germany was keen to extend her diplomatic tentacles across the rest of the continent too. The *New York Times* reported in 1913 that Berlin was upgrading the level of some of its diplomatic missions in the region. 'The rapid increase in the interest taken by Germany in Latin America is indicated by the provision made in the imperial budget of 1914 for the raising to the rank of full legations of the Minister residencies now accredited to the republics of Guatemala, Venezuela and Peru … ' wrote the newspaper's Berlin correspondent.[3]

The dominant influence on Francisco García Calderón was, however, French rather than German. He had begun the new century by entering the Faculty of Letters at San Marcos University where his father was then rector. The young Francisco quickly showed his talents as a thinker and writer, and with his younger brother Ventura and another student, José de la Riva Agüero, they formed a small coterie of student intellectuals. These three young men were, as mentioned in the previous chapter, part of the new wave of Peruvian thinkers, the 1900s Generation, who drew inspiration from Peru's pre-Conquest past and laid emphasis on the role of elites in society protecting the lower classes. After university the precocious Francisco began writing for the Lima newspaper *La Prensa,* his articles covering mostly politics and philosophy with an emphasis on European events.

This fruitful period for Francisco in Peru came to an abrupt end on 21 September 1905 when his father died. Deeply affected by the loss, the 22-year-old battled with depression, as he would do later in life. The following year the García Calderón family decided to leave Peru to start a new life in France. Francisco arrived in Paris on 28 April 1906 in company with his brothers Ventura, also a writer, José, an architect, and Juan, a doctor. Francisco was meanwhile made chancellor at the Peruvian legation in the French capital, a city where he was to spend much of the next 40 years of his life. Francisco plunged into the intellectual life of Europe with some enthusiasm, travelling to Britain and Germany and winning a prize in France in 1908 for his book *Le Pérou contemporain*. But the young man's focus was not just on his work at this time. In December 1908 he left Paris and returned to Lima to marry his fiancé, fellow Peruvian Rosa Amalia Lores, the following year.

Francisco García Calderón's international reputation as a writer and thinker continued to grow, as he wrote for newspapers in Cuba and Argentina as well as Peru. Then in 1912 his book on the democratic nations of his continent – *Les démocraties latines de l'Amérique* – was honoured with a preface by the then French Prime Minister Raymond Poincaré. This was not just an honour but an important contact; Poincaré would be President of France at the time of the 1919 Paris Peace Conference. In his preface Poincaré picked up on the Latin theme of the book and the need to protect Latin America from US cultural hegemony. 'Whatever the qualities of Yankee civilisation, it is not Latin civilisation, and M. Calderon would not have the latter sacrificed to the former,' writes the French premier. 'He implores South America to defend itself against the danger of a Saxon hegemony, to enrich itself by means of European influences, to encourage

French and Italian immigration, and to purify its races by an influx of new blood.'[4]

The book was seen as important not just in France – it was first published in French – but in Britain, America and Germany too, though curiously it was not published in Spanish until 1979. The book charts the history of Latin America from the Spanish conquests and the mingling of different races that had led to the development of different nation-states. Written just three years before the First World War broke out, García Calderón recognises three *perils* facing the Latin peoples of Latin America, namely the United States, Germany and Japan. On the German threat, the Peruvian points to the sizeable German population in Brazil, the country's investments in Central America and their acquisition of land, and building of both banks and railways. *The German Empire has the passions of a new people; the active faith, the practical Christianity, the cult of gold, the instinct of gigantic accumulations, of cyclopean enterprises, trusts, and combinations, and the optimism, the anxious desire to improvise the civilizing work of centuries by the pressure of sheer wealth.* However, unlike some in Latin America at the time, García Calderón saw the German threat as relatively remote. Even in Brazil, he notes, the numbers of German immigrants were small in relation to other populations. Meanwhile

'To save themselves from Yankee imperialism the American democracies would almost accept a German alliance ... everywhere the Americans of the North are feared.'
FRANCISCO GARCÍA CALDERÓN

Italian immigration, in particular, was growing, something that would help ensure the Latin nature of South and Central American nations. *The stiff-necked group of German colonists cannot vanquish these races, whose affinities are the same as those of the natives, and who bring overseas the sensuality of Naples and the commonsense of Milan.*[5]

For García Calderón, a more alarming threat or peril was Japanese domination of the Americas. A significant number of Japanese immigrants had already turned up along the Pacific coast of South America, notably in Peru itself. According to the author, the Japanese saw South America as being in their *sphere of influence,* and had similar designs on the continent to the Germans ... *we cannot deny that Japan has ambitious designs upon America,* he writes. And he makes it clear that for him, because of the enormous cultural differences, Japanese domination would be a bad outcome for Latin American nations. *The Japanese hegemony would not be a mere change of tutelage for the nations of America ... the ruling race, the dominant type of Spanish origin, which imposes the civilisation of the white man upon America, is hostile to the entire invading East.*[6]

Yet for all his concerns about the threat from Japan, and to a lesser extent Germany, García Calderón leaves little doubt about which threat he considered the most serious for Latin America. This was from the United States. *To save themselves from Yankee imperialism the American democracies would almost accept a German alliance, or the aid of Japanese arms; everywhere the Americans of the North are feared,* he writes. It was an interesting point of view given Peru's stance later in the First World War and also his and his own family's suffering at the hands of Germany. However, looking ahead to the likelihood of war in Europe, García Calderón saw Latin America less as a potential victim of North America and more as a potential saviour of classical European culture. *If in a Europe dominated by Slavs and Germans the peoples of the Mediterranean were forced to withdraw in painful exodus ... it is probable that ... the torch which bears the ideal of Latin civilisation would pass from Paris to Buenos Aires or Rio de Janeiro, as it passed from Rome to Paris in the modern epoch, or from Greece to Rome in the classic period. America, today deserted and divided, would save the culture of France and Italy, the heritage of the Revolution and the Renaissance, and would thus have justified to the utmost the fortunate audacity of Christopher Columbus.*[7]

In an attempt to keep that 'Latin civilisation' flourishing, García Calderón helped create a new magazine in 1912. Entitled *Revista de América*, its aim was to gather together the best writers from the 'Latin New World' in one non-dogmatic and free-thinking publication. More than ever, however, Garcia Calderón's time was divided between his writing and his more formal role as a Peruvian diplomat. In 1914 he was promoted to the position of First Secretary at the Peruvian legation in Paris. As war in Europe grew ever closer, the German 'peril' García Calderón had written about in 1912 was about to affect him more closely and personally than he could have imagined.

In Peru's neighbour, Ecuador, German commercial influence was also strong before and during the war. One British observer pointed out that 'practically the whole of the import trade of the country and a not insignificant part of the export trade ... [have long been] ... in the hands of the Germans and it must be admitted they [have] done everything to deserve it'. The army, too, was influenced both by the German and the Chilean military, and had even adopted the German goose-step march. Meanwhile the Ecuadorian government recruited German teachers in their schools and employed advisers from Germany to help on railway construction and other public works. And though France was far and away the leading buyer of Ecuador's main export – cacao – Germany was in third place behind the United States.[8]

The development of railways in South America at this time followed a familiar pattern. These projects usually involved foreign capital, investors and engineers, often German, British or American, and were designed to boost the country's economic efficiency. This was essentially the experience in Peru and Bolivia, for example. In Ecuador, however, the ambitious plan to build a railway between Guayaquil on the coast and Quito high up in the mountains took on an almost mystical dimension. The two cities had symbolised the divided nature of Ecuador since independence. Steamy, hot Guayaquil was the heart of the country's main export trade, a liberal stronghold and home to many of the country's wealthiest and most powerful businessmen and financiers. Conservative, devout Quito was the traditional seat of political power and the Church in the country, and was the power base of the country's aristocratic *sierra* landowners. To unite these two very different cities with a railway would surely change more than just travel times; it would help to bring together the country itself. That, at least, was the dream of José Eloy Alfaro Delgado, the veteran Liberal who had seized power in 1895 and who would twice be president. For him getting a railway built between Guayaquil and Quito became something close to an obsession. 'My dream … my only programme is concentrated in this one solemn word: Railroad,' he once declared.[9] There were of course plenty of good practical reasons for wanting to build a railway. Sending goods on the ramshackle road between the two cities was a very lengthy and expensive process. It has been estimated that sending a tonne of wheat from Quito down to the port city cost more at this time than sending a similar load from Australia to Europe. So with the support of much of the population and with the help of US backers, plans were made to build the line, and work eventually began in 1899.

One major problem was finance. Ecuador already had a so-called 'English' debt stretching back to independence days, and so in order to raise new capital the old debts were consolidated and new bonds issued. As before, many of the new bondholders were based in Britain. A second problem was logistical. Much of the land on the way to the Andes was soft, and deep stone foundations had to be laid to support the weight of the track and trains. Then there was the problem of building a railway to climb up the mountains without making it so steep trains could not use it. Given the scale of these difficulties, it is perhaps not surprising that the construction of the Guayaquil to Quito line suffered quite terrible problems. Up to 500 workers died in its construction, many from disease, including two senior construction engineers. The workmanship suffered too, as the US investor behind the project cut costs to save money. Even so, the budget spiralled out of control and the project ran well behind schedule. Alfaro was obliged to borrow extra money to keep his dream alive; meanwhile it was becoming increasingly likely that the British bondholders would struggle to get any return on their money.

When the railway was finally completed – Alfaro's own daughter América drove in the final, golden, spike on 17 June 1908 – the event was 'greeted with great enthusiasm' according to the *New York Times*. But what genuine joy there was at this historic event soon led to disillusionment. The state of the locomotives and carriages were poor, peasants in remote areas helped themselves to parts of the line, and journeys still took two days between the two cities. When within months of its opening the bubonic plague made its way up the line, the railway was unkindly dubbed '*la bubonica*'. More importantly in the long term, the financial black hole created by the construction project was to sour relations between the Ecuadorian government and foreign governments and investors – notably the many British bondholders of the Guayaquil and Quito Railway.[10]

Ecuador also had problematic relations with nations closer to home. In common with Peru, Ecuador seemed constantly in dispute over its borders, and indeed often with Peru itself. The two nations nearly came to war in 1910, for example, over a territorial dispute. The Ecuadorian government – more specifically Alfaro during his two terms as president – also got into trouble for trying to dispose of existing territory as well as retain it. This episode involved the Galápagos Islands off Ecuador's Pacific Coast. They are famous for the discoveries that Charles Darwin made there in the first half of the 19th century and are today prized as an ecological haven and tourist destination. But at the time these barren islands had defied most attempts to settle on them and had little obvious mineral wealth. Their main value lay in their strategic position, one made considerably greater after the Panama Canal was finally opened in 1914; the islands dominate the Pacific approaches to the canal. However, Ecuador lacked a navy able to protect the islands from attack, whether against a European power – France and Britain both expressed interest in acquiring them in the late 19th century – or a neighbour such as Peru. Alfaro twice made approaches to the United States to sell or lease the islands in return for money and/or a warship. However, when in 1910 news leaked out of the supposedly secret negotiations the Ecuadorian public was outraged. Protesters in Guayaquil were heard to shout 'Death to the Americans' and to their own president, and eventually Alfaro was obliged to drop the idea.

Another divisive issue in Ecuador at this time was Church-state relations. In Peru and Bolivia the role of the Church in political and social life was an important but not usually dangerous subject. But if there was one issue that divided Conservatives and Liberals in Ecuador – and it wasn't always easy to tell all their policies apart – it was organised religion and its role in society. In the second half of the 19th century the Catholic Church had played an important role in national life, notably under the pious García Moreno. Under him, being Catholic was an essential requirement for Ecuadorian citizenship. In contrast, Alfaro wanted to free the state from the Church's influence. The strength of feeling on both sides had been shown when Alfaro came to power in 1895. There had been a brief civil war, in which churchmen called for the masses to rise up against the Liberals, while for their part many clergy suffered harsh treatment. For more than a decade afterwards the dominant Liberal Party passed a series of ever more anti-clerical legislation, including kicking foreign-born priests out of the country, confiscating Church lands, removing the Church from involvement in state education and allowing civil marriages. The door was also opened to Protestant missionaries from the United States to operate in Ecuador, though their presence was often greeted with

THE PANAMA CANAL
The creation of the Panama Canal, which opened for shipping in August 1914, had an impact not just on world trade but on the geo-politics of the region. Even before it was created, the way the US project began sparked controversy in Latin America. The Panama Isthmus had been part of Colombia but when the latter refused to cede land to build a canal a revolt broke out in Panama, cheered on by the US. The Panamanians quickly declared independence, and the new country ceded land to build the new canal. For the US the canal increased the strategic importance not just of the Caribbean but also on the Pacific side – including Ecuador's Galápagos Islands.

opposition; some priests allegedly tried to incite their flocks to kill them. Meanwhile the Church itself was accused of funding violent rebellions against the Liberals in general and Alfaro in particular.

Alfaro's tough treatment of the church and his cavalier and brutal treatment of opposition – whether from newspaper editors or politicians – even alienated fellow members of the Liberal party, who believed he had betrayed the principles of the 1895 revolution. They were deeply unhappy, too, at the veteran's opportunist attempts to regain office. In 1911 Alfaro ended his term of office and left for Europe, but the man chosen to succeed him died. For the 'Old Battler' this seemed a golden opportunity to get back into power, and he immediately returned to Ecuador. But his fellow Liberal Leonas Plaza Gutiérrez, himself a former president, objected and a brief power struggle between the two factions ensued. Alfaro lost, and he, his nephew and a third man, General Pedro Montero, were arrested in Guayaquil. Montero was soon murdered by a street mob as violence broke out in the city. Alfaro and his nephew Flavio were meanwhile removed to Quito where they, too, met a grisly end. They were dragged from captivity by a mob, beaten, killed, and their bodies later mutilated. According to American newspaper reports at the time, another victim of the violence had his tongue cut out before being killed. It was also claimed that Montero was decapitated and had his heart torn out. Some supporters of Alfaro later claimed that Plaza was behind the murders – he took up office afterwards – though this did not stop Liberals from blaming the violence on the clergy and their preaching against Alfaro.

Witnessing the violence in Guayaquil, a member of the US Legation spoke of the 'brutal passions of a semi-civilised people', reflecting once again the rather jaundiced and often patronising view that many foreigners had of South American countries and their people. However, US representatives in the port city had often been at grave risk there – not so much from violence as from disease. During the 19th century yellow fever claimed the lives of more than one American diplomat, a death toll that continued into the early 20th century. Its reputation as a disease-ridden city had long been a deterrent to its growth; it was feared and avoided not just by foreigners but by people from Ecuador's mountains too. Alfaro tried to tackle the problem in 1906, asking for US assistance, but there was strong local opposition to outside interference. Gradually the situation improved, though even in 1916 some 166 people died from yellow fever and 345 from bubonic plague. It was not until 1919, with the help of the Rockefeller Foundation, that yellow fever was finally eradicated. The last case was reported on 22 May of that year. At last the 'fear of visiting Ecuador ha[d] disappeared' and visitor numbers to the city grew.[11]

During this time of Liberal rule and sporadic violence, Ecuador's future delegate at the Peace Conference, Enrique Dorn y de Alsua, was in the rather calmer environment of Paris. Since his work in helping organise Ecuador's display at the Paris Universal Exhibition, Dorn had become the Chargé d'Affaires at the Ecuadorian legation in France, and was establishing important contacts in the upper echelons of Parisian society. He was also one of the men whose photographs were chosen to illustrate a large advertorial that appeared in *The Times* on 7 May 1913, which gave a rather rosy view of life and investment prospects in Ecuador. In particular the article – 'The Awakening of Ecuador' – seems to have been a lengthy plug to encourage readers to put money in gold mining in and around Zaruma. Dorn, meanwhile, represented his country in 1907 at the Second Hague Conference held to discuss international relations and agreements; useful experience for someone who would attend the Paris Peace Conference.

Bolivia's future delegate was meanwhile enjoying a high-profile political career as president of his country. Ismael Montes held the office twice from 1904 to 1909 and for a further four years from 1913. He has been described by the historian Fredrick B Pike as the 'dominant political figure presiding over Bolivia's era of progress'.[12] By the time he became president for the first time, Montes had experienced the highs and the lows of Bolivian politics. In early 1898 he had been arrested and exiled for his views as a member of the Liberal opposition, and had then played a prominent role in the fighting that led to the Liberal revolution. Under Pando's presidency the forceful and respected Montes was made Minister of War, where he was credited with modernising the army and boosting its pay. He was well-placed to take over as president from Pando in 1904, and like his predecessor presided over a mini-boom, overseeing the building of new railways, for example. A victim of political excesses in the past, Montes was not above bending the rules. When his elected successor died before being able to take up office Montes engineered himself another year as president, a move that attracted bitter criticism.

Even when Montes did eventually leave office for the first time in 1909, his influence remained huge. He followed what was by now a well-worn path for former South American presidents in travelling to Europe, where he represented his country in both Paris and London. Here he helped raise loans to establish Bolivia's Central Bank and to construct a new railway back home. Yet despite Montes' undoubted importance as a politician, military leader, lawyer, diplomat, and latterly as a financier, the real reason why Bolivia progressed so well at this time lay not in national politics or ideology – but in mineral wealth, most especially in tin.

The wealth that lay below its surface had always been key to the country's development, first as a Spanish colony and later as an independent republic. Initially the most important metal was silver, and places such as Potosí became synonymous with silver mining. In the second half of the 19th century the silver-mining industry was one of the cornerstones of Bolivia's relative prosperity, and helped rescue the country's fortunes after the disaster of the War of the Pacific. However by the end of the 19th century the world silver market was in decline and by the end of the century prices had collapsed. Fortunately for the country – and certainly the wealthier elites – tin more than filled the gap. Much of the western world was going through industrial growth and demand for tin – which Bolivia had in abundance – grew significantly. Fortunately, too, tin was often mined in the same areas as silver, which meant that the infrastructure modernisation and railway-building that had been carried out to help the silver mine owners also benefited many of the new breed of tin mine owners. The figures show the rapid nature of the boom; from 1892 to 1896 the country exported 31,583 tonnes of tin, but this figure leapt to 245,364 tonnes for the period 1917 to 1921. By 1900 tin already accounted for 41 per cent of all Bolivian exports, a figure that reached 72 per cent in 1920. The age of tin had arrived.

There were key political differences between the silver mine owners and the tin mine owners, however. The former were strongly identified with the Conservatives in Bolivia and had become directly involved in national politics. In contrast, the tin mine owners were generally linked with the Liberals, but felt no need to become personally involved in the political game themselves. This was left to a coterie of lawyers, economists and technical advisers whose 'job' it was to handle the politics and ensure that government policies met the needs of the mine owners – for example, building railways, creating financial institutions and facilitating investment. These people made up what was known in Bolivia as the *Rosca* or 'Screw', a group who effectively ran the country on behalf of the mine owners. Another difference was in the aspirations of the mining companies that produced the tin. Unlike the silver owners, some of the tin barons went on to become important players on the world business scene. By far the most important of these was Simón Iturri Patiño.

Patiño was born in 1860 in Bolivia's Cochabama Valley, but his exact origins are uncertain. Some say he was mixed race with Indian and Spanish heritage, others that he was of pure Spanish origins. He certainly came from a modest background and began working in the mining industry, as a clerk in a store. Legend has it that he accepted the deeds of an old mine as payment for a client's modest debt and was fired for doing so. All he was left with were the deeds to the old mine – which turned out to be rich in tin. In 1912, however, his secretary Ernesto Buschenhagen – Patiño apparently spoke very little English – told the *New York Time*s a rather more prosaic story, claiming that Patiño had been a modestly successful general storeowner in Oruro who in 1894 had been given the chance to buy a mine for $18,000. He and his wife pooled their savings, sold the store and bought the mine – which thanks to the purchase of modern equipment and the new owner's attention to 'the smallest detail' quickly turned a profit. Buschenhagen then explained the secret of

Patiño's great and rapid success. 'You see, in Bolivia the cost of production is very low. Labour is cheap and the mines are very rich. The only thing was to find a market.'

Patiño proved very effective at doing just that. From around 1900 to 1910 Patiño bought up as many mines as he could and by 1906 was able to establish the Banco Mercantile in La Paz, supposedly with capital of $25 million. Later he turned his attention overseas, buying up foreign tin smelting plants. In time he became one of the wealthiest men in the world and was known as the 'Tin King'. Patiño lived abroad for many years, in Paris, New York and Buenos Aires, and for a period represented his country at international conferences in France in the 1930s. The family became well-known in elite circles; his son Antenor married María Cristina de Borbón y Bosch-Labrus, the Duchess of Dúrcal, who was related to the then Spanish king, while his granddaughter Maria Isabel Patiño later married the French/British financier James Gold-smith. A sign of the close links between the tin barons and the Liberal Party is underlined by the fact that one of the lawyers who worked for Patiño for a period was Ismael Montes – the man who would twice be president of the country as well as its delegate to the Paris Peace Conference.[13]

Despite the wealth in the country created by the tin barons, and the relative stability of the political scene, these were nonetheless not years of unbridled success for the Liberal Party, especially in foreign relations. There was a rubber boom in the Amazonian regions at the time, and Bolivia's land along the Acre River attracted many migrants from neigh-bouring Brazil. President Pando hoped that the United States would back Bolivia against Brazilian claims on the area, but Washington was more interested in remaining on good terms with Bolivia's giant neighbour. The result was that in a short armed conflict the Bolivian military were defeated and at the 1903 Treaty of Petrópolis La Paz had to cede 73,726 square miles of the Acre lands to Brazil, an area roughly the size of the whole of Uruguay. Then Montes' first administration signed a treaty in 1904 formally ceding to Chile the entire coastal strip that it had lost to her neighbour in the War of the Pacific, in return for a new railway line from Arica on the coast to La Paz. Despite signing this treaty, however, Montes and Bolivia were never reconciled to the loss of this outlet to the ocean, and would later seek to claim a new, more favourable outcome – using the venue of the Paris Peace Conference.

Unlike the three Andean Republics, Uruguay had few border problems at this time. Nor did it follow the liberal economic politics witnessed in Ecuador and Bolivia. Instead, and improbably, the small republic steered a rather different course towards becoming Latin America's first welfare state. The man behind this startling transformation was José Batlle y Ordóñez. Batlle's father had been president at the end of the 1860s and José himself, a journalist and politician, soon became a leading light in the Colorado Party. He had made his name as a vocal opponent of the military dictatorships that had dogged the country, and for advocating labour reform. To publicise his views he used the columns of his own *El Dia* newspaper, often in very forthright, aggressive terms. Having briefly been interim president in 1899, Batlle was chosen to be the country's president in 1903. Shortly before he was elected he unveiled his programme, which was to enact social reforms to help the lot of ordinary people, to seek peaceful relations between the two rival parties and to reform and modernise public administration.

Sections of the Blanco Party were bitterly opposed to Batlle. Aparicio Saravia, who as a youth had apparently taken up arms against Batlle's father when he was president, soon led a revolt. Saravia had gathered his own private army, which had strong support in parts of the Uruguayan countryside. By early 1904 his forces were in open conflict with those of the official Uruguayan government led by Batlle. The decisive showdown came in September of that year at Masoller, in the north of the country close to the border with Brazil. Saravia's rebels were defeated and he himself was shot and wounded; taken across the border into Brazil by friends, he died ten days later. On 24 September 1904 the Aceguá peace accord was signed. It was the end of the last civil war in Uruguay.

After completing his first term in office Batlle went on to serve a later, second term as president from 1911 to 1915. But his reforms and force of personality were felt right throughout this period, up to and after the First World War. It was a time of quite remarkable change, especially given the lack of social legislation in other Latin American nations at this time. A divorce law gave more freedom to women, secondary schools were set up across the country and – eventually – an eight-hour working day was established. Later, pensions and paid holidays were granted too, and income tax abolished for low-paid workers. There were wide-ranging financial and economic reforms, including the setting-up of a state insurance bank in 1912 and, in the same year, a state company to control the generation and distribution of electricity. Uruguay also scoured the world looking for good ideas about how to improve society – and then adapted them to suit their own requirements. Health was one such area. 'Uruguayans were clearly adept at participating in international health networks and adapting foreign innovations to serve local needs,' notes one academic. An example of their success was in fighting child mortality. By 1913 a doctor involved in child care, Julio

Bauzá, even felt able to claim that the country no longer had to pay much attention to the issue as its child mortality rates were lower than those of Chile, Russia, Germany and France. 'The truth is we are in an enviable position for a myriad of European and American countries,' he said.[14]

Another area where Batlle himself looked to innovate using overseas examples was in the country's system of government. One of the themes of his career was a desire to prevent the possibility of strongmen or *caudillos* governing Uruguay, as they had done for much of the 19th century. When he left office for the first time the former president sailed to Europe to study systems of government. He was particularly taken with the Swiss model in which a one-man system had been replaced with a more collegiate style of leadership. Back in Uruguay and back in office in 1911, Batlle eventually tried to establish a similar system for his own country. It was a deeply controversial idea that sparked opposition not just among the Blancos, but among some sections of his own Colorado party too. It would take until 1919 before the measure would formally be adopted – and only after Batlle had threatened to run for the presidency for a third time.

Though the remarkable Batlle fought all his life against *caudillos*, and is rightly credited with establishing Latin America's first welfare state, he was no colourless technocrat. One of the most striking features about his life was that he fought at least five personal duels and either issued, or was issued with, challenges on many other occasions. Often he was challenged by an opponent whom he had attacked in one of his newspaper columns. In 1920 he killed one opponent, Washington Betrán Barbat, whose son was later to be president of Uruguay. Duelling was illegal in the country, and as president, Batlle intervened to prevent it when he could. But he also knew that if he wanted to continue his vehement criticism of society's problems and be listened to with respect, he himself could not avoid having to fight a duel over his articles. Though his double life as polemicist and president led to criticism at the time, there is no doubting the stature of Batlle and the astonishing changes he helped to bring about in Uruguay at this time.

While Batlle was busy reforming the country, its future Paris delegate Juan Buero was honing his skills as a lawyer, diplomat and speaker. In 1908 he organised the first Congress of American Students. This was held in Montevideo, which because of Uruguay's status as a small, peaceful buffer state between Brazil and Argentina was often chosen as a 'neutral' venue for international gatherings. Two years later the talented Buero was made assistant director of the International Office of Students. After completing his studies in 1910, he was made a professor of international law at both the Commercial High School and the School of Law and Social Sciences in Montevideo. The busy young man also had time to fit in a career in journalism, editing *El Tiempo* newspaper and later *La Razón*. By now Buero was attracting the attention of the government and in 1913 he joined the Foreign Ministry. In the same year he also became an MP for the department called Thirty-Three – in honour of the heroes of Uruguayan independence. It was a dazzling start to his career for the young man, still only 25, one that would continue to blossom in the coming years.

Diplomatic and cultural ties between Uruguay and Europe remained close at this time, helped partly by the large Italian and also Spanish immigration the country enjoyed. There were also smaller populations of Britons, German and French immigrants. A curious visitor to Uruguay in 1910 was

Georges Clemenceau, the man who would be the dominant French politician at the Paris Peace Conference – himself a proficient duellist. His brief visit was part of a longer trip to Argentina and Brazil, but the veteran French politician nevertheless spent enough time in Montevideo to draw a few conclusions about the country. It also seems likely that he met Juan Buero. Though he does not mention him by name, Clemenceau refers to a 'young journalist, a Deputy who has spent a long time in Paris and is generally considered to be a coming man'. The description seems to match Buero fairly well. The Frenchman was impressed with Uruguay's education system, liked the city's geography – and admired the beauty of the city's women. And commentating on the country's violent recent past, Clemenceau conceded that Europe had not always set a great example. 'We must admit that Uruguay is not without a show of reason when she replies by throwing up at us the floods of blood that we have shed in the course of our civil wars, and that down to our most recent history... . In Uruguay the first indication of this new order of things will be the suppression of revolution. Before this comes to pass there will be great changes on both sides of the ocean, in the reflex action of humanity and, in a less degree, in its reasoning consciousness,' he wrote.[15] Such great changes were, indeed, just a few years away.

3

The Republics and the War 1914–18

The outbreak of war in Europe in August 1914 came as little surprise to the governing circles in the South American republics. Their representatives in Paris – for example García Calderón for Peru and Dorn y Alsua for Ecuador – had been passing back intelligence on the deteriorating situation in the Balkans and the worsening relations between Britain and France and Germany. Nonetheless, the brutal nature of the conflict was still a shock. Many of the educated and political classes in Peru, Bolivia, Ecuador and Uruguay looked to Europe and especially France as their cultural home. When they were not running their own countries, many of these elites spent a good deal of time in the old continent 'escaping' – sometimes literally – from the occasional unpredictability and capriciousness of their own countries. Yet here were France, Germany and Britain embroiled in a bloodier war than anything seen on the battlefields of South America.

Of course, for the majority of the population of the South American republics the conflict meant little or nothing. The war was being waged in a faraway place of which some had never heard and few would ever visit. But the Europeans themselves did not see Latin America as remote or unimportant to the war. For one thing there was the food and raw materials that Central and South America had to offer. Uruguay provided shiploads of beef to Europe, Argentina provided beef and wheat, Ecuador sold cacao, Brazil coffee, and Bolivia its tin. Peru meanwhile supplied sugar, though this trade was disrupted early in the conflict when the British bought up large quantities from the Far East. Peru's cotton, too, was in strong demand from the Allied powers from 1915, as the usual supplies from Egypt became harder to source.

Continuing this trade meant that the shipping lanes had to be protected. The opening of the Panama Canal on the eve of war had already had a major impact on these routes. Ships plying their trade between the Pacific coast of South America and Europe no longer had to take the long and difficult route around Cape Horn to the south. They could now pass through the canal instead. This meant that not only were the traditional transatlantic routes from Argentina and Uruguay of strategic importance to both the Allies and the Germans, so too were the entire Pacific coast and the coastal waters of Central America and the Caribbean. On a military and strategic level, Latin America was thus far from irrelevant to the European combatants. While no one may have seriously expected a Latin American state to join in the fighting, the Europeans saw the region as a place where they could win hearts and minds with the aim of boosting or protecting vital trade links and using the republics as sources of supply bases, while denying them to the enemy. To this limited extent, Latin America thus became a proxy battlefield between the Germans and the Allies.

The significance attached to Latin America by the British is shown by its determination to push pro-British propaganda into the region. A 1917 memorandum reveals how the British Foreign Office's News Department used a 'subsidised' Reuters service to send its 'propaganda' messages to Buenos Aires, from where they were relayed to Brazil, Uruguay and Chile. The document betrays more than a touch of cynicism and opportunism. 'The South American papers are always anxious for material, and all, except those actually under German control, will print very nearly everything that is sent them by cable. A similar service on a smaller scale has lately been started for Central America and Mexico, with a distributing centre at Panama,' it states. It adds: 'We also send a weekly cable meant primarily for the obscurer places – containing a summary of the British military news, with a few items of general interest, for the previous week.' A number of articles were dispatched in Spanish, though some were sent in English – for the local British representatives to work on: '… in most of the capitals the Ministers have a little local committee, which arranges for the translation of such articles and their insertion in newspapers.' The memorandum dryly notes that articles with photographs for illustrated newspapers are 'very successful' and that Brazilians apparently had an 'insatiable appetite' for pamphlets produced by the British. Clearly, however, the government propagandists knew where to draw the line. 'I am glad to say that we subsidise no newspaper in the continent,' notes the author. In general it was felt that most work was needed in Central America, where pro-German feeling was at its strongest. 'Propaganda in South America is not nearly so necessary as in some other countries, feeling either being quite strongly for the Allies (as in Brazil), or at any rate not hostile,' it concludes.[1]

Though the British may have felt they had the upper hand in the propaganda battle by early 1917, this did not mean the Germans were without friends in South America. Peru, in particular, was worried about the strong German influence in Chile, the country with which it had fought a disastrous war just three decades earlier. German immigration to Chile had been high – certainly compared to countries such as Peru – and there were a number of important immigrant communities in the country. A number of German businesses and businessmen were also operating in Santiago and the key port of Valparaiso.

It was this last group that most actively promoted the German cause at the outbreak of war, according to some observers. 'They represented the aggressive and militant Germany of 1914 and scrupled at nothing to further the interests of their native land,' noted one. As elsewhere in South America, sections of the Catholic clergy were also pro-German. But it was in the military and especially the army that Berlin's influence in Chile was strongest; the South American country had been developing links with the German military since the 1870s. 'The army is pro-German through and through,' noted one German writer with approval. The Chilean army in turn had influenced the Ecuadorian military. So it is little wonder that Peru, which had hosted a French military mission since 1896, was alarmed about potential German military meddling to both north and south involving neighbours with whom it historically had tense relations. In particular, there was concern in the streets of Lima in November 1914 over rumours that Germany had built a naval station near Valparaiso. In fact, such fears were largely unfounded. Chile's main aim during the war was to maintain the strictest neutrality so that it could benefit from the widest sales of its copper and nitrates. And when in December 1914 Chile placed restrictions on the refuelling of foreign warships in her ports, the German minister in Santiago gave the news a frosty reception.[2]

Peru's own sympathies at the onset of war clearly lay with the Allies, largely due to its close ties with Britain and especially France. German sympathies, such as they were, were largely confined to sections of the clergy. For their part, the country's intellectuals were generally supportive of the Allies, as were the main newspapers. Yet, like other South American countries, Peru determined to remain neutral at the start of the conflict, even though it did not formally issue a decree to that effect. One reason for this was that Peru's economy had been badly hit in the downturn in world trade preceding the war, especially by falling sugar prices. The start of war then caused European credit to dry up. The last thing the country now needed was the potentially disastrous economic disruption that could occur if it took sides. At the same time, the country's government at the start of the war was cautious in matters of foreign affairs. President Leguía had been replaced in the 1912 elections by Guillermo Billinghurst, a descendant of a British sailor who had fought for South American independence in the early 19th century. A wealthy man, Billinghurst was a populist, erratic and prone to emotional outbursts. He tried to court the masses and became known as 'Big Bread' Billinghurst for his championing of cheap food for the workers. But his overtly populist style and unpredictability alarmed many, and he was overthrown by an army rebellion. On 15 May 1914 a new provisional president was named. Colonel Oscar Benavides, a hero of the War of the Pacific, was a somewhat reluctant politician, and not someone inclined to make bold decisions when it came to Peru's involvement in the First World War.

Peru's initial policy was to seek pan-American co-operation

among its neutral neighbours to ensure that trade was affected as little as possible by the conflict. It hoped that the opening of the Panama Canal would boost commerce and was keen to ensure nothing interfered with this. Within a few weeks of the start of the war Peruvian diplomats in America sought to use the Washington-based Pan-American Union to co-ordinate a common approach to the war. In particular Peru was pushing for an enlarged neutrality zone around member states' shores. Other Latin Americans initially reacted positively, and by the end of the year members had agreed to set up a neutrality commission. Ultimately, however, the initiative got nowhere, despite protestations of support from various South American states. One reason was the sheer complexity of reaching such an agreement among so many different countries, many of whom had shared intense rivalries and a history of disputes with each other. Another reason was the attitude of the United States. Though the machinery of the Pan-American Union was based in Washington, this did not mean the United States saw the organisation as key to its diplomacy. The US certainly paid little attention to the idea promoted by Peru.

THE UNITED STATES, LATIN AMERICA, THE CARIBBEAN AND THE WAR
America's neutrality at the start of the First World War chimed with the prevailing view among most Latin American nations that the European conflict had little to do with them. When Washington changed policy in 1917 and eventually declared war, the countries whose foreign policy it effectively controlled, such as Panama and Cuba, quickly followed suit. American involvement also made it less risky for countries such as Peru, Uruguay and Bolivia to break relations with Germany. But for a mixture of nationalistic reasons, commercial considerations and anti-American sentiment three major regional powers – Mexico, Chile and Argentina – stayed neutral, as did Colombia and Venezuela. The main umbrella organisation representing nation-states in the Americas at this time was the Pan-American Union, forerunner of the current Organisation of American States.

This is not to say, however, that the United States and its new president Woodrow Wilson, who had taken office in 1913, were indifferent to Pan-American agreements. Indeed, they positively welcomed them – as long as they were on their terms. President Wilson was already at work on his own idea for cross-continental co-operation. This was a Pan-American 'liberty pact', an American idea that pre-dated his administration but one that Wilson adopted with some enthusiasm. The idea was in essence an extension of the Monroe Doctrine of 1823, which stated that all of the Americas were closed to European colonisation and that any intervention in the continent would be regarded as a threat to American security. That declaration was intended to keep European powers out of Latin America, or the United States' 'back yard'. The Monroe Doctrine was seen as a policy that defended the United States' interests rather than those of other countries in the continent; the aim of the liberty pact was to extend this idea among the other nations of the Americas, guaranteeing each other's independence and borders by stating that any incursion into one state would be seen as a threat to the others.

A 1914 draft of the proposed pact's most important article spoke of 'mutual guaranties of political independence under republican form of government and mutual guaranties of territorial integrity'. In the end, Wilson's plans came to nothing. Partly this was because of the hostile reaction to recent US military interventions in Nicaragua and Haiti, partly because Chile feared such wording could compromise its position in Tacna and Arica and partly because when the US entered the First World War in 1917 this dramatically changed the diplomatic mood in the Americas. Yet the draft pact resolutions were not entirely wasted. The wording on independence and territorial integrity was to make a reappearance in Article 10 of the League of Nations Covenant agreed at Paris in 1919, even if the words 'republican forms of government' were removed. In fact, it has been argued that Wilson's Pan-American policies – from his military and political interventions in the Caribbean, Central America and Mexico to his plans for a Pan-American liberty pact – helped form part of his agenda at the 1919 Peace Conference, and that 'Latin America served as Woodrow Wilson's proving ground for the basic principle of the League of Nations'.[3]

Another important reason why it was hard to get the Latin American republics to sign up to Pan-American agreements was that it was hard for them to feel under imminent threat from the war in Europe. Trade was initially disrupted – though as the war continued commercial opportunities for some nations in South America actually grew, especially with the US – and the Allies and Central Powers plotted and intrigued on the continent. But there was little or no likelihood that the Americas would become an actual battleground for the European powers.

The possibly of military action along South American coastlines receded after defeat of the German naval squadron commanded by Admiral Maximilian Graf von Spee. Von Spee's force had been in the Pacific when war broke out and he decided to head for Germany via Cape Horn. *En route* he planned to disrupt Allied shipping as much as he could. To begin with he was successful, defeating a British force at Coronel off the coast of Chile in November 1914, an outcome that stunned the British Admiralty. Von Spee was also in radio contact with Germans on the Chilean mainland. The following month, however, von Spee launched a raid on Port Stanley on the Falkland Islands, only to encounter a superior British naval force. Von Spee's ship was sunk and both he and his two sons lost their lives.

In Europe itself Francisco García Calderón was busy at his desk in Paris, representing Peru's interests and sending back the latest thinking on the progress of the war. One of his younger brothers, José, meanwhile, had chosen to get more involved in the conflict. Like a number of young men from the Americas, he enlisted in the French Foreign Legion and took part in the fighting. José was killed at the Battle of Verdun in 1916 and Francisco was devastated by the news. Shortly after the end of the war he wrote a philosophical book about the nature and purpose of war in general and of the recent conflict in particular. It may have been an attempt by García Calderón to make sense of the death of his brother, and the book was dedicated to the *Memory of my brother sub-lieutenant José García Calderón* who had *died on the field of honour at Verdun on 5 May 1916.*[4]

Enriquez Dorn y de Alsua was also involved in wartime diplomacy. Though the independently wealthy Dorn cut something of a dandyish figure with his immaculate grooming and well-cut suits, he was nonetheless a shrewd and experienced diplomat who, thanks to the time he had spent in France, knew his way around the corridors of power in that country's government. His experience was called on early in the war when Ecuador quickly became involved in a dispute with Britain and France. As early as 17 August 1914 the Ecuadorian government formally declared that it would remain neutral and that it would abide by the terms of the 1907 Hague Convention – which set out laws on respecting the neutrality of non-combatant countries and the responsibilities of neutral countries not to aid and abet combatants during wartime – at which Dorn had represented the Quito government. Ecuador's move was an unsurprising one, and in line with both that of other Latin American countries and of the United States. However both British representatives in Ecuador – A E Rennie and Lucien Jerome – and the French resident minister, Henri Francastel, greeted this declaration with suspicion. In contrast, the German resident minister, Heinrich Rohland, accepted Ecuadorian neutrality with good grace and played a rather more astute diplomatic game.

The French and British diplomats soon found a cause over which they could seek to justify their suspicions about Quito's motives. The Galápagos Islands form one of the most strategically sensitive areas along the Pacific coastline of South America. In September 1914 the German cruiser *Leipzig* arrived to refuel with coal from two transport ships, one German, the other Norwegian. The cruiser's captain also took advantage of the stopover to land the crew of a sinking British ship that it had picked up. In early October the British sailors were sent to mainland Ecuador where the regional governor informed the authorities in Quito of what had happened. The governor also warned the Ecuadorian minister of foreign affairs Dr Rafael Elizalde that he 'suspected' that the German navy was 'attempting to utilise this archipelago as a base for its raids'. Elizalde himself informed Jerome and his French counterpart of the report, stressing it was simply a 'suspicion' but that if there were any substance to it then the Ecuadorian government would lodge a formal protest with the Germans.[5]

According to the Ecuadorians, Jerome accepted this statement at face value and was apparently satisfied with it. However, his report back to London put the matter in a very different light. So much so, in fact, that it was announced in the House of Commons as a 'fact' that the Germans had set up a naval base in the islands. Officials in London also claimed that Ecuador had failed to meet British and French requests for proper control over the wireless station at Guayaquil to stop it from being used by the Germans for intelligence purposes. The Ecuadorians denied this. They admitted that the British and French had *claimed* that German diplomats were making improper use of the wireless stations. But Ecuadorian officials said that the two men had also accepted that the Ecuadorians had not been aware of this unauthorised use. Now, however, the French and British authorities used this and the naval base issue to criticise Ecuador for an alleged breach of neutrality. To make matters worse, the British government had taken the view – on Jerome's advice – that it would be pointless to raise the matter again with the Ecuadorians directly. Both the British and French governments now asked the United States to intervene in the matter, and to seek an assurance of strict neutrality from the authorities in Quito.

This tactic did not go down well in Ecuador, which felt that the representatives of France and Britain had been both unfair and misleading in the way they had presented the two issues. The authorities also felt particularly aggrieved that the French and British had dragged the US into the affair. Foreign Minister Elizalde wrote to the British and French expressing his unhappiness, while Dorn y de Alsua worked hard in Paris to reassure the French authorities about Ecuador's behaviour. In a series of letters and face-to-face meetings with French foreign ministry officials at the Quai d'Orsay, Dorn reinforced Elizalde's message and made it clear that Ecuador was strictly neutral in the war. He also made the same points to the British ambassador in Paris. Dorn's efforts paid off, and by early 1915 the French and British considered the matter closed. The Ecuadorian diplomat was able to write back to Quito that the French Foreign Minister Théophile Delcassé had recognised Ecuador's *good faith* throughout the controversy. This acceptable end to the diplomatic contretemps was later said to have been 'due in considerable part' to Dorn y Alsua's expert lobbying.[6]

An investigation by the Ecuadorians had meanwhile found that the *Leipzig* had overstayed her time in the Galapagos Islands, even though there was no evidence of a German base there. The Ecuadorians sent a message of protest to Berlin about this violation of her sovereignty. Germany was not the only culprit. Two British ships and a Japanese cruiser were also said to have overstayed their welcome in Ecuadorian territorial waters and diplomatic messages were duly despatched to their capitals too. Then in 1916 Germany's representative in Ecuador, Heinrich Rohland, left, and his duties were taken over by Berlin's man in Peru, a Dr Perl. Perl, however, did not travel to Quito to present his diplomatic credentials, as is usual practice across the world. Instead, another German diplomat Wilhelm Muller arrived from Seattle to inform the Ecuadorians that he would be taking over Rohland's day-to-day duties. Quito considered this a breach of protocol and refused to recognise Muller's position. Though a seemingly trivial affair, this episode marked a decline in relations between Ecuador and Germany, a deterioration that would one day help persuade the South American country to end its neutrality.

Despite a gradual shift in the country's diplomatic position towards the Allies – one that largely mirrored that of America – there was still considerable pro-German sympathy on the ground in Ecuador. This was certainly the view among members of the British community in the country. Partly this was because of the way German businessmen had built up links with local traders; this meant that when Britain tried to restrict German trade in South America as in the rest of the world, for example through the infamous Black List – which placed trade restrictions on any countries thought to have links with the enemy – Germans were not the only ones to suffer. 'The Ecuadorian shopkeeper had been made to feel his dependence on the German,' noted one British observer, ' ... he consequently resented bitterly the restrictions placed upon German trade during the warm for thereby *his* gains were gone.' Then there were the clergy. Though the Liberals were still in power and had passed anti-clerical measures, this did not mean that the Catholic Church had lost all influence, and certainly not its hold over many ordinary people. British observers believed there was at least one good reason why many in the Church in Ecuador would champion Germany against Britain and especially France. In the early 20th century an anti-clerical movement in France had resulted in a series of laws that attacked religious orders and laid the foundations for the country's modern secular state. The sight of French secularists undermining the role of the Church naturally struck a chord in Ecuador, where the clergy were facing a similar battle. The local clergy in Ecuador accordingly set about anti-French propaganda work with some gusto. 'Not even the Germans themselves could vie with the Roman Catholic clergy as German propagandists,' noted *The Times*. The writer pointed out that until the outbreak of war Germany had been less well-known than China in a country where France was historically a 'household word'. Yet the 'common masses' and the 'more fanatical of the upper classes' had become enthusiastic supporters of the German cause once the conflict began. '"France needs to be punished for her apostasy ... " was the argument used,' said the British observer.[7]

The war also had an impact on the country's crucial cacao industry. Up until the First World War Ecuador had enjoyed something of a cacao boom, and by 1914 was producing about 45,000 tonnes a year or 15 per cent of world demand. The resulting revenue led to banks being set up and also funded lavish lifestyles for some landowners. Some of these had left their lucrative crops in the hands of managers and set off for extended stays in Europe. There were accounts of ships arriving at Guayaquil from France or the US laden with fine goods, and of small boats taking caseloads of brandy up to small communities where well-off cacao owners lived. One of the most colourful stories involved a landowner who bought an aristocratic title in France and styled himself Conde Mendoza in Ecuador. One doubtless apocryphal tale is that the count kept a large crocodile on his plantation, and if a worker misbehaved then the hapless man was thrown to the animal to feed upon. It is certainly true that these were tough times for workers in Ecuador, cacao boom or not.[8]

The war ended this mini-boom. Cacao was not deemed an essential commodity by the European powers and demand fell. Disease, too, badly affected the cacao crop. The downturn put even greater financial pressure on a government that was always hard-pressed for money and that had become dangerously dependent on this one crop. This lack of state revenue had a knock-on effect on an issue that was a constant source of tension between Ecuador, the US and overseas investors – the Guayaquil and Quito Railway. The company was a US firm, though many of the bondholders investing in it were British. Under the agreement that the company boss Archer Harman had signed with the Ecuadorians, the government had to pay the bondholders if the railway failed to make a profit. As discussed earlier, this was something the railway had singularly failed to do. Ecuador, however, said it had no obligation to pay the bondholders, claiming that Harman had cheated them and that it had no money anyway. There was also a dispute about who should pay for repairs to the line.

The nationality of the investors and the railway owners naturally drew the British and US governments into the dispute. This caused tensions not just between the three countries but also between private British and American citizens. The British bondholders believed that the legal agreements they had signed meant that they had first claim on any income that Ecuador made from its customs duties – and with which it was supposed to pay the bondholders. These investors were therefore horrified to learn that an American firm, Speyer and Co., had loaned the Ecuadorian government £300,000 and that the Ecuadorians had agreed to 50 per cent of its customs duties as security for the loan in return. This was the very money to which the many British bondholders felt they were entitled and of which they had so far not received a penny.

An angry meeting of holders of 'First Mortgage gold bonds of the Guayaquil and Quito Railway Company' was held at the Council of Foreign Bondholders in Moorgate Street, London, in February 1916. The gathering voted unanimously to take legal action against Speyer and Co to recover the money that the US firm had received from Quito. At the same meeting the bondholders made clear their unhappiness at the way they had been treated by the authorities in Ecuador. A Mr T H Tatham of the bondholders' council declared that its members had 'done an enormous amount of work … in bringing great pressure to bear on the Ecuadorian government in order to make them see the short-sightedness of their policy in their present treatment of the bondholders'.

He said the council had received 'great sympathy and help' from both the Foreign Office in London and the State Department in Washington. This included a firm commitment from the US authorities. 'The American Government has informed the Ecuadorian Government that they would not see their way to help them get a loan until they settled their differences between themselves, the bondholders and the railway company,' he told the meeting to cheers. Unfortunately the situation was not quite so easily resolved. The Ecuadorians were convinced by now not just that the railway had become something of a blight on the country but that they had been fooled by the company which built it. They were adamant they would not now pay foreign investors for the privilege of having been duped.[9]

It was only when the fall in cacao sales during the war began to hit home that Ecuador was reluctantly forced to react to the bondholders' demands. The US, well aware that it was by far the biggest market for Ecuadorian cacao, began to put concerted pressure on Quito. The War Trade Board began to place restrictions on the importing of cacao and warned the authorities in South America that unless the American (and other) bondholders received money this approach would get even tougher. The Ecuadorian government tried to stand its ground, and one diplomat told the Americans: 'I would rather burn all the cacao of Ecuador than accept this US imposition.' But eventually, by October 1918, after the US made good its threats and interrupted the loading of cacao onto ships in Guayaquil, the Ecuadorian authorities gave way and paid some money to bondholders. This was far from being the end of the matter, however, and the issue would hang over Ecuador's participation at the Paris Peace Conference.[10]

In Bolivia the start of war occurred during the second presidency of Ismael Montes. Having spent part of his time in between terms in Europe, he already had a clear grasp of the diplomatic situation there leading up to the war. It was no great surprise when Montes and his government made clear at the start that the country would remain neutral in the war, in common with the rest of the continent. As Montes had spent time in London and Paris it is reasonable to assume that much of his private sympathy lay with the Allies. Moreover, his Liberal Party was a supporter of pro-trade and financial policies that met with approval in the neutral United States. However, some sections of the Bolivian population betrayed pro-German sympathies. In 1913 Bolivia imported more goods from Germany than from any other country, and was indeed the only Latin American country for which Germany was the top importer. This was largely thanks to the number of German companies in La Paz and elsewhere in the Andean country. The army, too, had strong links with the German military. A German military mission headed by General von Kund had left Bolivia just two months before the start of the war.

However, for Montes and his government the pro-Berlin sympathy of parts of society was not their top priority. The pre-war economic crisis had hit the country badly, reducing income and causing nervousness among the country's wealthy elites. New attempts to modernise the country's finances and economy now met with considerable opposition, including within the ranks of the Liberal Party. This division – exacerbated by a feeling among some that Montes should not have sought a second term – eventually led to a formal split. In 1914 half of the Liberal Party left to form the new Republican Party. By the time Montes handed power to his successor, the

British-educated economist José Gutierrez, in 1917, the Liberals' grip on power was already beginning to loosen, opposition was growing, and rumours about rebellions and revolts began to multiply. The hardships suffered by the country's workers because of the disruption of the economy during the war also added to the growing sense of tension, as did the assassination of former president José Pando in June 1917. Rightly or wrongly, the Liberal Party was widely blamed for his murder. Montes himself was criticised for being unyielding and inflexible in his wielding of power, prompting a congressional inquiry into alleged excesses of his rule after he left office in late 1917.

In Uruguay the man in charge of his country when war broke out was José Batlle, the dominant figure in Uruguayan politics during the first half of the 20th century. His administration was quick to declare the country's neutrality, setting out strict guidelines on the length of time that warships from belligerent countries could spend in Uruguay's ports and restrictions on the use of radio communications in Uruguayan waters. As a small country buffered between the two regional giants Argentina and Brazil, Uruguay always had to show caution in its foreign policy.

Nonetheless, there was little doubt that the sympathies of most in the small republic were with the Allies and especially the French. As Clemenceau had discovered a few years before, Uruguayans were profoundly interested in France, its ideas and history. This strength of feeling – especially prevalent among the political classes – was exemplified by Congress's decision in 1915 to make Bastille Day a national holiday in Uruguay. Juan Antonio Buero, now a parliamentarian, shared this pro-French sentiment – as one might expect given his birth – and his rousing speech on the topic on 10 July 1915 was later described as brilliant. The only real cause of irritation with the Allied side during the war was provoked by Britain's Black List, intended to hamper Germany's trade efforts. In Uruguay, as in other parts of Latin America, these wartime trade restrictions angered many business people who felt they were too harshly and indiscriminately applied and hit firms with the most tenuous connections to Germany. Otherwise the mood was solidly pro-Allied, promoting one German writer to note that in South America 'Uruguay is the only country in which is to be found a clearly expressed hostility to Germany'. Buero, meanwhile, was heavily involved in regional diplomacy. In 1914, as an official in the Foreign Ministry, he had been a member of the official Uruguayan delegation that had travelled to Argentina after the death of its president Roque Saénz Pena. Later he was made chairman of the foreign affairs committee in the House of Representatives and became close to Foreign Minister Baltasar Brum, with whom he had worked in his student days in Montevideo.[11]

The mood towards the war and Germany hardened in Uruguay and the rest of Latin America early in 1917, when Berlin adopted a policy of unrestricted submarine warfare to impose a blockade around Britain, France and Italy. This was a turning-point in the South American view of the war. Until now, while passions might have become inflamed by the horrific accounts of battle or the sight of Allied or German ships passing through regional ports, the war remained remote. Now, however, even shipping from neutral countries such as the South American states was under direct threat from German submarines. Berlin's policy also triggered a response from the United States, the region's superpower. On 3 February 1917 Washington severed diplomatic relations with Berlin, followed by a declaration of war on 6 April. These actions sent shockwaves through the diplomatic corridors of the South American republics, as the countries faced up to the unwelcome prospect that they themselves might have to choose sides in the conflict. The European war had just grown a lot closer.

Uruguay's reaction to Germany's threat to neutral shipping was a toughly-worded response complaining about breaches of international law. Montevideo said it reserved the right to employ appropriate measures to defend itself. Foreign minister Brum also went out of his way to praise Woodrow Wilson's stance when the US announced its diplomatic breach with Germany. However, as a small and militarily weak country, Uruguay felt little inclination to make the first move among Latin American countries to change its neutral status. When the US finally declared war on Germany, Montevideo scrupulously reaffirmed Uruguay's neutrality. The mood was already changing to Uruguay's immediate north, however. Brazil had lost shipping to German attacks and on 1 June broke off diplomatic relations with Germany.

This action from its powerful neighbour galvanised the mood in Uruguay. While still stopping short of cutting relations with Germany, it issued a bold declaration about how the Americas should respond to the German menace. In a statement of 18 June 1917 the government in Montevideo said: ' … No American country, which in defence of its own rights should find itself in a state of war with nations of other continents will be treated as a belligerent … '. This 'unique manifestation of Pan-American idealism' – in effect Uruguay was appealing to a continental solidarity that was much talked about but rarely acted upon in practice – struck a chord with fellow republics. The Bolivian government applauded the declaration, which it said reflected its own views. Meanwhile Brazil congratulated her 'sister republic' on such a striking affirmation of Pan-Americanism at a time when the 'fundamental principles of civilisation imperilled in the Old World seek shelter and equilibrium among the free peoples of the two Americas'. The United States, which had hoped that the South American nations would follow its path in at least breaking off relations with Germany if not declaring war, also welcomed the declaration, and Uruguay's words won fulsome, almost gushing, praise from Secretary of State Robert Lansing.[12]

Uruguay soon had a chance to back up its fine words with some action when it welcomed a US naval squadron to Montevideo, and the American sailors were greeted with great celebration. Yet President Viera and his government had still not actually broken off relations with Germany. One reason was that Uruguay still hoped for a concerted policy from fellow Latin American countries, possibly even an agreement on breaking off relations with Germany at the same time. But Uruguay also remained nervous, even now, about the implications for the country if it were to make a unilateral declaration. In particular President Viera and his government were concerned about the sizeable German community that lived in southern Brazil, close to the border with Uruguay. This population had been growing since the 19th century, had its own newspapers, and had shown sympathy for Germany's position during the war. The Uruguayans were fearful that Berlin might provoke an uprising among this German community and spark an invasion of Uruguay with the aim of seizing its ports. Such was the depth of concern that during the autumn of 1917 President Viera contacted Argentine president Hipólito Irigoyen to seek assurances of Buenos Aires' support in the event of such an invasion, particularly in providing arms and ammunition. Argentina confirmed it would come to Uruguay's aid in such circumstances.

In reality the likelihood of such an invasion ranged from the wildly improbable to the virtually inconceivable. The German population in southern Brazil, while sympathetic to the mother country's cause, showed little inclination to take up arms to support Berlin. Nor, apart from some lurid rumours, was there was much evidence that Germany was poised to intervene militarily in the area. Nonetheless, Uruguay's fears were not entirely fanciful. During the summer of 1917 the German minister in Buenos Aires, Karl von Luxburg, had sent home a series of rather loose-tongued despatches about German interests in southern South America. In one of them Luxburg referred to his country hoping for a 'reorganisation of south Brazil'. Others referred to the Uruguayan government itself. The contents of some of these explosive texts – which were intercepted by the Allies – were not made public until some time later. In February 1918 President Viera told the country's Congress that the government had serious suspicions both that Germany was planning to provoke an uprising in southern Brazil and that an 'invasion of our territory was planned from the north'.[13]

By the time President Viera made these startling remarks, Uruguay had finally broken off relations with Germany. This

ARGENTINA AND THE WAR
Argentina maintained a policy of strict neutrality during the entire First World War, though a significant part of public and intellectual opinion was sympathetic to the Allies. When he became president in 1916 Hipólito Irigoyen doggedly pursued the same neutral line, even after Germany began its submarine blockade of Europe early in 1917 and Argentine ships were sunk. Meanwhile the country's economy prospered in the war, thanks to its exports of beef and grain. As a neutral country Argentina was not invited to the Paris Peace Conference but did become a member of the new League of Nations.

happened in early October 1917 after a meeting of Congress and an appeal from the President himself. The vote to break off relations was carried by a large majority. The change of mood in Uruguay was largely due to the fact that it was now clear Brazil was going to declare war on Germany; a belligerent Brazil on military alert would reduce the risk of a German uprising there, it was felt. Brazil duly declared war late in October.

The Peruvian decision to break off relations with Germany also occurred in October 1917 but in its case the motive was rather more clear-cut. Back in 1915 Peru had confiscated the German liner *Luxor* when the ship refused to leave Callao port within the specified time period. This act, though, was carried out to protect Peru's neutrality. Soon after Germany declared its policy of unrestricted submarine warfare in January 1917 however, a Peruvian cargo vessel, the *Lorton*, which was carrying nitrates to Spain, was sunk by a German submarine off the Spanish coast. The Peruvian authorities were naturally outraged – it was a neutral ship carrying goods to neutral Spain – and demanded not just an apology but compensation. Germany, which insisted that the nitrates were bound for France, was reluctant to provide either.

A lengthy diplomatic wrangle ensued between the two nations, with the Peruvian authorities – and public opinion – contrasting the sympathetic way that Germany had dealt with Argentina after sinking one of its vessels with its handling of the *Lorton* affair. But there was another factor at play in Peruvian diplomacy. During an address to Congress in July 1917 President Pardo went out of his way to approve comments from President Wilson on liberty, justice and self-determination. His country, said Pardo, could not be 'indifferent to the words of President Wilson', especially as 'in a war fought not long ago' the country had 'sacrificed for these ideals the blood of her sons, her wealth and her hopes for the future … '. It was clear to all that Pardo was referring to the War of the Pacific, and the subsequent dispute over Tacna and Arica with Chile. Peru wanted the US as an ally in its row with Chile, and approving President Wilson's words was an attempt to win Washington's support. Earlier in the year, when the US had declared war on Germany, the Peruvian government had also withheld from reaffirming its neutrality, afraid that to do so might irritate the US. It was these two issues, the failure of Germany to meet its demands over the *Lorton* and Lima's hopes for US backing against Chile, that led Peru to break off relations with Germany early in October 1917.[14] However, Peru's attempts to remain in the US's good books were not always successful. The Peruvians had already interned ten German ships that were in their ports. The Allies were desperate for all the shipping they could lay their hands on, and the Peruvians were in no position to carry out expensive repairs on vessels that had lain idle for some time. Eventually a deal was struck in which the US would lease the vessels for the remainder of the war. However the US believed that Peruvian haggling delayed the lease agreement unnecessarily, and Secretary of State Robert Lansing sent a rather terse message to Peru's diplomats, suggesting that the delays had created an unfortunate impression in the US.

Despite pockets of pro-German sentiment, Bolivia broke off relations with Berlin in April 1917, after the extension of submarine warfare but well before Uruguay and Peru. La Paz's frustrations with Germany had been apparent since 16 March 1916 when a Dutch ship the *Tubantia*, was sunk by a German submarine in a foggy North Sea as it headed for Buenos Aires. On board were the Bolivian minister to Berlin,

Luis Salinas Vega, and his family. Although the crew and passengers were all rescued before the ship went down, the incident provoked an outcry in Bolivia. Yet it was not until 13 April the following year that Bolivia finally sent its German minister packing and officially broke relations. The timing was significant; less than a week before Bolivia's decision, the United States had declared war on Germany.

Bolivia's move away from neutrality had, however, begun in January 1917 when Woodrow Wilson told the US Congress that all nations had the right to an outlet to the sea, either by the cession of territory or by the 'neutralisation of direct rights of way under the general guarantee that will assure peace'. To a country such as Bolivia, which had lost its access to the sea in the War of the Pacific, this was an alluring message. If the world's most powerful man was proposing such a doctrine, it seemed logical for Bolivia to do all it could to earn his favour. Little wonder, then, that deference to the US had quickly become of 'paramount importance' to Bolivian diplomats, or that the rupture of relations with Germany flowed on so quickly from Washington's entry into the war. Ismael Montes, president at the time, was also an admirer of President Wilson.[15]

The last of the four South American nations to sever relations with Germany was Ecuador. In its case, too, there was also a desire to please the United States. Indeed, later, during the often tricky negotiations between Quito and Washington over the Guayaquil and Quito Railway in 1918, one of

'Ecuador ... is morally on the side of the Allies.'
ENRIQUE DORN Y DE DORN

the reasons why Ecuador felt aggrieved at the US's aggressive stance on the issue was that it felt it had already shown its friendship towards the United States by having broken off relations with Berlin. In 1917 Ecuador also suggested a congress to discuss the issue of South American neutrality, now that the German submarine threat had grown and the US had entered the conflict. Only Mexico expressed serious interest in taking up the offer, however.

Yet throughout most of 1917 Ecuador had still shown little inclination to alter her neutral status, despite internal criticism; the former foreign minister Rafael Elizalde, for example, was one who held the view that the country was dragging its feet. In August President Baquerizo Morteno once again reiterated his country's neutrality in his address to the country's Congress. Behind the scenes there were some hints Ecuador might be prepared to move, and Enrique Dorn y de Alsua in Paris briefed the French press that Ecuador *which regards herself as united through sentiments of solidarity with the republics of America which have entered the war, is morally on the side of the Allies.* Yet even after Peru and Uruguay ended their neutral status, Ecuador did not budge.[16]

The catalyst for Ecuador's change of heart was as much an affair of national honour as a shift of diplomatic policy. When Peru expelled its German minister, Dr Perl, the latter decided to go to Ecuador, where he was also technically the senior German representative. However, as he had never previously turned up to present his credentials, the Ecuadorian authorities were in no mood to accept him now. They made it clear via diplomatic channels that if he did try to visit the country, he would not be officially received. Meanwhile the junior German representative in Ecuador, Dr Muller, had not been recognised as a diplomat either, because of the breach in formalities committed by him and Perl. Much to the annoyance of the Quito government, Muller nonetheless insisted on calling himself the *chargé d'affaires*. He then gave further offence when in a letter of condolence over the death of a popular archbishop in early December 1917 he signed himself 'chargé d'affaires of Germany, though not yet recognised', and at the funeral insisted on sitting with the rest of the diplomatic corps. When Muller gave no sign of wanting to apologise for his actions, Foreign Minister Carlos Tobar y Borgoño decided enough was enough. On 7 December he issued a note among the accredited diplomatic corps announcing the formal break in relations with Germany. Interestingly, Tobar y Borgoño effectively backdated the break by claiming that relations between the two nations had been suspended for some time. In any case, thanks to this somewhat technical diplomatic squabble, Ecuador had now joined Peru, Bolivia and Uruguay, and at last had come down on the side of the Allies. It now remained to be seen what, if any, benefits these countries would get from their actions.[17]

Dr Juan Antonio Buero as a Uruguayan senator in 1942.

II

The Paris Peace Conference

4

Paris 1918–19

As the end of the war approached, the Allied nations in Europe realised they urgently needed to improve relations with Latin America. One by-product of the war was a growth in South American economic ties with the United States at the expense of Europe, while the opening of the Panama Canal had also altered trade patterns. South American countries were very aware, too, that the sudden disappearance of credit from countries such as Britain – which their economies had come to rely on – had hit businesses and workers hard. A growing sentiment of economic nationalism led some Latin American observers to warn against an over-reliance on overseas finance and trade in the future. Political and business leaders alike also resented some of the harsher measures taken by the Allies to counter enemy trade, most notably Britain's unpopular Black List.

The need to rekindle strong links between Britain and Latin America – where there were still millions of pounds invested – prompted the despatch of a trade mission from London in April 1918. The British Special Mission to South America, as it was called, visited Chile, Bolivia, Peru, Ecuador and Brazil as well as other countries, and was led by experienced diplomat Sir Maurice de Bunsen. Its explicit aim was to restore and extend the political and economic ties that Britain had enjoyed with Latin America before the war, a time when the City of London had been a major source of credit and investment for the continent's nations. The fact that Britain did not show its wartime ally the United States the courtesy of informing it of the mission underlines the fact that it was aware who its main economic competitor in the region now was. Back in 1914 the focus had been on competition from Germany; now, with hopes the war would finally be over soon, attention switched to the United States. Understandably, many in Washington saw this mission – which took place while Americans were still dying on the Western Front – as yet another example of underhand British attempts to undermine US trade in South America. US representatives had already complained that the British Black List operated as much against American interests in Latin America as it did against German interests – even after Washington joined the war. Yet though the Bunsen mission was warmly welcomed, a number of British businessmen in South America and members of the mission itself doubted whether Britain had the political and commercial structures to regain its once predominant position.

In Latin America itself there was concern that Pan-American policy towards the war lacked cohesion. In November 1917 John Barrett, the director-general of the Washington-based Pan-American Union, warned that unless there was proper co-ordination of those Latin American nations which were at war – chiefly those in Central America under the influence of the US plus Brazil – and those who had broken off relations – Bolivia, Ecuador, Peru and Uruguay – then German influence could yet play a decisive role in the region.

German diplomacy and 'propaganda' could 'completely offset and nullify all the apparent advantages of Pan-American co-operation and support in this war,' said Barrett, who urged the creation of a Pan-American Advisory Council whose role would be to counter German propaganda which he said was 'growing every day bolder and more desperate'. He added: 'Something now should be done or there will be danger of trouble.' The US government saw the sense in this argument. However, it had already proven very difficult to organise any meaningful common policy in relation to the war. The situation was complicated by the fact that three of the most powerful Latin American nations – Chile, Argentina and Mexico – remained neutral throughout. Indeed, in American and some European eyes, the last two especially exhibited some pro-German sympathies, or at least anti-US sentiment.[1]

The different stances adopted by Latin American countries during the war – ranging from belligerence to full neutrality –

THE SOUTH AMERICAN VIEW OF PRESIDENT WILSON
The Latin American nations' view of Woodrow Wilson was coloured by the gap they saw between his rhetoric and his country's actions. Wilson spoke about the need for self-determination, but his (albeit reluctant) interventions in Mexico – under Wilson American troops seized the port of Vera Cruz in 1914 and two years later American troops entered the north of the country, both times in response to internal disorder and to protect American interests – caused controversy and unease in the region. On the whole, however, his championing of international rights found favour in many quarters; in April 1918 even Argentina's government – not at the time noted for its pro-US stance – praised Wilson's words and deeds. Many countries in the region saw in Wilson's proposed League of Nations an organisation that would help protect them.

also made it hard for the victorious Allies to agree on how to handle the region once the fighting officially ended on 11 November 1918. Which countries, if any, should be invited to the planned Paris Peace Conference? From the outset it was clear – at least to Washington – that Brazil would be accorded a place at the conference table. Brazil had been the only South American country to declare war on Germany, and though its role in the war had been negligible – restricted to the sending of a field hospital and a small squadron of ships which arrived in European waters just as the war ended – American President Woodrow Wilson was keen that its useful ally should be rewarded with a place at the table.

The situation regarding Bolivia, Ecuador, Peru and Uruguay was very different. These countries had severed relations with Germany in 1917 but none had declared war. Peru and Uruguay had suffered some minor losses at sea and the four nations' move to end neutrality had made it easier for Allied shipping in the region, but it was stretching a point to suggest either that the countries had made any meaningful contribution to the war effort or that they had suffered great hardship as a result of their 'sacrifice' in severing diplomatic relations. So when in late 1918 diplomats from the three great Allied powers – France, Britain and the United States – began casting around to see who should be invited to the forthcoming Conference in Paris, these four countries were hardly top of the list. In fact, even in early January 1919 it was by no means certain that Peru, Ecuador, Bolivia or Uruguay would be invited to take any meaningful part in the Conference. Aware of this doubt, their foreign ministries had begun lobbying the Great Powers, asking for a place at the table.

An example was the efforts made by Juan Carlos Blanco, Uruguay's minister in Paris. On 7 January 1919 he sent a lengthy letter from the French capital to the British Prime Minister David Lloyd George. Blanco itemised the support that Uruguay had given to the Allies during the war, including:

making its ports available for Allied warships; allowing them
to use its telegraphic services; patrolling its waters searching for enemy submarines; impounding German vessels in its
ports; providing food for the peoples of Europe; and agreeing
with Brazil that it would fight against any 'German agitation'
in the south of that country. Finally, wrote Blanco, by its 'constant propaganda' Uruguay had 'helped maintain confidence
and morale in South America'. The only reason Montevideo
had not despatched troops to Europe was that 'circumstances'
had not allowed it. Blanco insisted such actions set it apart
from neutral countries with which it was now 'in 'discord'
– meaning relations were strained – because of its stance.
Moreover, Uruguay was still in potential danger from Berlin.
'If Germany had the means, she would doubtless attack
Uruguay, in order to demand an account for it's [sic] acts and
to recover her confiscated property.' Blanco warned that if his
country did not get 'solid and decided support' from Britain
and her Allies then its 'international situation' would be 'difficult'. And he told the British premier: 'If Uruguay is not
present at this Conference, she will find herself absolutely
isolated … '. Similar letters were sent by Uruguayan diplomats to the other Great Powers.[2]

Peru, too, was wondering whether it would be represented
at Paris. The Peruvian foreign ministry politely but pointedly
asked the US State Department whether it had any information about countries that had broken relations with Germany
– such as Peru – being invited to the Conference. Bolivia was
also pressing its claim to be at the Parisian get-together,
though the tone it struck in its attitude towards at least one
of the Allies – Britain – was not always tactful. In late 1918
the Bolivian foreign minister Alberto Gutiérrez wrote to
the British authorities demanding that wartime economic

restrictions – imposed under the Black List – be lifted immediately. Moreover, the Bolivian minister wanted Great Britain
to pay his country compensation for losses suffered as a result
of British wartime measures. The demands got a cold and
disdainful reception from the British Foreign Office's man in
Bolivia, Godfrey Haggard, who called them 'wholly unjustifi-
able'. In implicit criticism of earlier attempts by London to
mollify the Bolivians, Haggard also noted that showing 'any
consideration' was 'thrown away on these people' and that
when the Bolivians were in the wrong they should be 'made
at once to feel that H.M. Government have no intention of
tolerating their attitude'.[3]

The participation of both Bolivia and Peru in Paris was
also complicated by the perennial problem of Tacna and
Arica, and by Bolivia's continuing demand to be allowed to
regain access to the sea. During 1918 tensions between Chile
and Peru over Tacna and Arica had increased and anti-Peru-
vian violence broke out in the Chilean town of Iquique. By
the beginning of January 1919 there were reports of thou-
sands of Peruvians fleeing the area, and claims of brutality;
for example, in Arica a prominent Peruvian lawyer, his wife
and children were said to have been beaten with boathooks
before being thrown into the water. They were rescued and
put aboard a boat carrying other refugees to safety. Ironically, it seems as if the approaching Peace Conference may
have played a part in escalating this latest tension. Peru had
already been encouraged by President Wilson's plans to create
a League of Nations at the Conference. Lima was further
inspired by the anticipated restoration of Alsace-Lorraine
from German to French ownership, which was expected to be
agreed in the forthcoming Peace Conference. Peruvian diplomats argued that this strengthened their own case for having

Tacna and Arica restored to its ownership – something the Chileans naturally disputed.[4]

Bolivia was also linking its claim to an outlet on the Pacific Ocean to the forthcoming talks in Paris. It helpfully suggested that one way to solve the Peruvian-Chile dispute over the coastal strip was simply to give it Arica. It then suggested that La Paz should send a delegation to Washington and/or Paris to discuss this issue. The Bolivians again drew inspiration from President Wilson himself. His Fourteen Points, outlined in a speech in January 1918, included the assertion that Serbia should be given access to the Adriatic

> 'It would be a major injustice to confuse our situation with that of countries that were simply neutral.'
> ENRIQUE DORN Y DE ALSUA

Sea. If Serbia could gain a maritime outlet, then why not Bolivia too? That was the tone of a note sent in January 1919 by Ismael Montes, who had become Bolivian minister to London and Paris the year before, to the British and French foreign ministries and Peace Conference officials. Interestingly, the British – despite their impatience with La Paz over other issues – backed the claim, somewhat to Washington's annoyance, which saw it as interference in a purely American affair. Neither Wilson nor Secretary of State Lansing wanted Bolivia to send a delegation to Paris or Washington to discuss the issue. Wilson and his delegation now knew that any lofty pronouncement by the President regarding one part of the world was likely to be seized on by other countries to further their own claims. This was something both Peru and now Bolivia had done successfully – effectively by quoting Wilson's words back at him.

Ecuador's man in Paris had also been hard at work, lobbying for Ecuador to be admitted to the Conference. Having

PRESIDENT WILSON'S FOURTEEN POINTS, 8 JANUARY 1918

The program of the world's peace, therefore, is our program; and that program, the only possible program, as we see it, is this:

I. Open covenants of peace, openly arrived at, after which there shall be no private international understandings of any kind but diplomacy shall proceed always frankly and in the public view.

II. Absolute freedom of navigation upon the seas, outside territorial waters, alike in peace and in war, except as the seas may be closed in whole or in part by international action for the enforcement of international covenants.

III. The removal, so far as possible, of all economic barriers and the establishment of an equality of trade conditions among all the nations consenting to the peace and associating themselves for its maintenance.

IV. Adequate guarantees given and taken that national armaments will be reduced to the lowest point consistent with domestic safety.

V. A free, open-minded, and absolutely impartial adjustment of all colonial claims, based upon a strict observance of the principle that in determining all such questions of sovereignty the interests of the populations concerned must have equal weight with the equitable claims of the government whose title is to be determined.

VI. The evacuation of all Russian territory and such a settlement of all questions affecting Russia as will secure the best and freest cooperation of the other nations of the world in obtaining for her an unhampered and unembarrassed opportunity for the independent determination of her own political development and national policy and assure her of a sincere welcome into the society of free nations under institutions of her own choosing; and, more than a welcome, assistance also of every kind that she may need and may herself desire. The treatment accorded Russia by her sister nations in the months to come will be the acid test of their good will, of their comprehension of her needs as distinguished from their own interests, and of their intelligent and unselfish sympathy.

VII. Belgium, the whole world will agree, must be evacuated and restored, without any attempt to limit the sovereignty which she enjoys in common with all other free nations. No other single act will serve as this will serve to restore confidence among the nations in the laws which they have themselves set and determined for the government of their relations with one another. Without this healing act the whole structure and validity of international law is forever impaired.

VIII. All French territory should be freed and the invaded portions restored, and the wrong done to France by Prussia in 1871 in the matter of Alsace-Lorraine, which has unsettled the peace of the world for nearly fifty years, should be righted, in order that peace may once more be made secure in the interest of all.

IX. A readjustment of the frontiers of Italy should be effected along clearly recognizable lines of nationality.

X. The peoples of Austria-Hungary, whose place among the nations we wish to see safeguarded and assured, should be accorded the freest opportunity to autonomous development.

XI. Rumania, Serbia, and Montenegro should be evacuated; occupied territories restored; Serbia accorded free and secure access to the sea; and the relations of the several Balkan states to one another determined by friendly counsel along historically established lines of allegiance and nationality; and international guarantees of the political and economic independence and territorial integrity of the several Balkan states should be entered into.

XII. The Turkish portion of the present Ottoman Empire should be assured a secure sovereignty, but the other nationalities which are now under Turkish rule should be assured an undoubted security of life and an absolutely unmolested opportunity of autonomous development, and the Dardanelles should be permanently opened as a free passage to the ships and commerce of all nations under international guarantees.

XIII. An independent Polish state should be erected which should include the territories inhabited by indisputably Polish populations, which should be assured a free and secure access to the sea, and whose political and economic independence and territorial integrity should be guaranteed by international covenant.

XIV. A general association of nations must be formed under specific covenants for the purpose of affording mutual guarantees of political independence and territorial integrity to great and small states alike.

floated the possibility to Quito that the country could be invited to the table, Enrique Dorn y de Alsua received the not entirely helpful instruction: 'Take the initiative if you believe it will be successful.' Dorn spoke to the French international lawyer Edouard Clunet, who was involved in setting up the Conference. Relaying the conversation to his diplomatic bosses Dorn said: *I observed to Señor Clunet that it would be a major injustice to confuse our situation with that of countries that were simply neutral, and that while it might appear that we were simply in a position between belligerents and neutrals our sympathy was obviously on the side of the Allies. I also pointed out the risk we were running in the event of a German victory.*[5] By early January there were signs that the Great Powers were prepared to admit to the Conference those South American countries that had broken relations with Germany. The US in particular lobbied on behalf of its fellow nations from the Americas, and was keen that this be known in diplomatic circles. Washington did not want to let a chance to win easy plaudits from its Latin American neighbours go begging.

The decision on the final status of all the countries attending Paris for the Peace Conference was taken shortly before the Conference was formally opened on 18 January 1919. The French Foreign Ministry had already written to delegates from 29 countries, nations that might claim to have been on the Allied side. But this did not necessarily mean they would all be invited to take part in the Peace Conference itself. (Just to add to the confusion, this was still technically designated as a preliminary conference that would give way later to a full Peace Congress, though in the end the Conference just carried on.)

The status of Ecuador, Bolivia, Peru and Uruguay was still unclear right up to the eve of the opening. One factor that helped swing things in their favour was that Germany itself objected to them being invited, on the grounds that Uruguay and Peru had not declared war but had still gone ahead and seized German ships. The other key factor was the influence of President Wilson, who argued that countries such as Peru and Uruguay should be given access to those meetings where the subject at hand was of interest to them. Otherwise, so his argument went, they would be reduced to the same status as the neutral countries, whose representatives could merely be summoned at the request of the Conference organisers. Wilson's view prevailed.

The delegations to the Peace Conference were now divided into three separate categories. The first and by far the most important were the 'belligerent powers with general interests'. These were the United States, France, Britain, Italy and Japan. Next came the belligerent powers with particular or special interests, a group that included those Central American nations that had been at war, plus Brazil from South America. Finally the third group was designated as powers in a 'state of diplomatic rupture with the enemy powers'. This group contained Bolivia, Ecuador, Peru and Uruguay. As with some of the second category, these four countries only had the right to one delegate each at the Conference. However, this meant just one delegate at a time – delegations could contain more than one delegate in their 'team' to allow specialists to take part in relevant discussions.

In Peru's case, it chose three delegates. The lead delegate, and the one officially announced to the diplomatic world on 16 January 1919, was Francisco García Calderón. Although he had represented Peru in Paris during the war, becoming minister in March 1918 and then being awarded the Légion d'honneur by France, García Calderón had recently been made minister in Brussels. However, as a fluent French speaker who knew Paris and French politics intimately, the erudite, experienced diplomat was an obvious choice for the position. His contacts were excellent too: Raymond Poincaré, the current French President, had written a preface to one of García Calderón's books just before the war and it was he who welcomed delegates at the opening of the first Plenary Session at 3 p.m. on 18 January.

The other two Peruvian representatives were both diplomats. Carlos González de Candamo, also the son of a diplomat, was born in London in 1871 but spent his later childhood in Paris, where his father was Peruvian minister. In contrast with the cerebral García Calderón, Candamo was an accomplished sportsman. He captained the Racing Club side when it became the winner of the first French rugby championship in 1892 and later represented his country at fencing in the 1900 Olympics in Paris. Candamo was also a talented tennis player. He had been invited to become a member of the International Olympic Committee in 1909. Like his father, Candamo now worked as a diplomat. Though in many ways very different from García Calderón, they had one thing in common: Candamo, too, had lost a member of his family during the war, his brother Gaspar having been killed in October 1915. The third member of the team was Victor Manuel Maurtua, an expert on the War of the Pacific and the intricate details of the subsequent dispute between Peru and Chile.

Uruguay, like Peru, also had three delegates in Paris. Jacobo Varela Acevedo, who was born in 1871, had been his country's Foreign Minister for a brief, controversial period before the First World War. A veteran diplomat, he described himself as a staunch defender of Pan-Americanism. Another member of the team was Juan Carlos Blanco, another diplomat who was already the Uruguayan minister in Paris and who would carry out much of the paperwork of the delegation. However, it was Juan Antonio Buero who was to prove the most high-profile of the Uruguayan delegates during the Peace Conference.

Like the other two delegates, Buero was fluent in both English and French and he also knew Paris well. Indeed, as he left Montevideo with his wife Alda Brum – the sister of Balthasar Brum who was about to become president – to sail to Genoa, from where they took a train to the French capital, Buero was able to reflect on the significance of his destination. 'Paris was the city where he was born, so it was very special for him to return to that city,' said his son Dr. Enrique J. Buero. When they arrived in Paris Buero and his wife initially stayed at the Saint James d'Albany hotel in Rue de Rivoli; accommodation was hard to find because of the huge demand. Later the couple found a more permanent place to stay in a very comfortable flat in Rue La Boétie in the capital's 8th arrondissement, close to the Avenue des Champs-Élysées. Buero found it exhilarating to be in Paris at this time. Despite the privations caused by the war and its aftermath, the city was alive with activity linked to the Conference. His son described what his father saw and felt at the time. 'Paris was wonderful, although there was a shortage of many basic things,' said Dr Enrique Buero. 'My father saw delegates from different countries in the different boulevards of this impressive city and there were lots of social activities in Paris in those days, all related to the Peace Conference.'[6]

Buero loved being surrounded by so many great names on the world stage, including Woodrow Wilson, David Lloyd George and Vittorio Orlando, even if they were not all that approachable. 'Meetings with the big personalities were thrilling for my father – for example, the French President

Monsieur Raymond Poincaré opened the Elysée Palace to the different delegations,' said Dr Enrique Buero. 'Formal and distant, he exchanged greetings with the Uruguayan delegation. When told that a street was to be named after him in Montevideo he said "Men are nothing, nations are everything".' However, Buero and the rest of the delegation's meeting with Georges Clemenceau – who had recently been to Montevideo – was much warmer. 'Just tell me anything you need in Paris – I know the support your country gave in the war,' he told them. Despite the gravity of the Paris meeting, there were also lighter moments for Buero and his wife. The diplomat traveled around the city in a horse and carriage, with the blue stripes of the Uruguayan flag proudly fluttering from it. Buero was amused to note that people constantly confused it with the Greek flag.[7]

Bolivia had one official delegate to the Conference, Ismael Montes. He was the only one of the delegates from the four Spanish-speaking South American republics to have been his country's head of state and this, coupled with his recent experience as minister to London and Paris, enhanced his standing as a delegate. He was also, at the age of 57, older than men such as García Calderón, Candamo and Buero. Montes also had a busy family life, having produced 12 children with his wife Bethsabé Montes, who came from a well-known Bolivian family and who was later president of that country's Red Cross organisation. As president in April 1917 it was Montes who had broken off relations with Germany, and he was also the man who had felt compelled to sign the infamous treaty in 1904 that had formally ceded the country's coastline to Chile. If anything this made Montes even more determined to help win that land back.

His background gave Montes a very broad perspective

of the key issues affecting his country at the Conference. In his messages back to La Paz, Montes shows himself to have been a shrewd observer, with a keen lawyer's eye for potential contradictions in an argument. For example, though he had written to the French government on 14 January stating that Bolivia claimed its right to a port in line with Woodrow Wilson's declarations, Montes was concerned that this line was at odds with the previous arguments Bolivia had used in claiming right to a link to the sea. He was also worried that raising the issue in the way it had with America, France and Britain, and then at the Conference, sent out the wrong signals. *We would not have been able to justify the fact – which doubtless would have seen in a poor light – that we had brought before a foreign, international body a case in which we had not sought an agreement between the parties themselves and which they should have been informed about beforehand,* he wrote. *Consequently, the key thing, before anything else, was and is to discuss our aspirations with Chile and Peru.* The former president also made it clear that Bolivia's claim that they had a right to a port under the Wilson doctrine – in which he specifically mentioned Serbia – was getting rather lost in the *furore* caused by Italian concerns over Yugoslavia (of which Serbia was a part). Yet he was equally clear that Bolivia had to pursue its case to get Arica with real conviction. *It is vital that the world gets used to seeing this as a matter of the greatest importance for Bolivia and not, as has been the case till now, as a dispute between Chile and Peru,* he wrote. *Having told Europe that we think we have superior*

'It is vital that the world gets used to seeing this as a matter of the greatest importance for Bolivia and not, as has been the case till now, as a dispute between Chile and Peru.'
ISMAEL MONTES

claims than Peru or Chile to Tacna and Arica, and then not to
sustain that position against the countries concerned, might
bring into question our stance and even lose the sympathy we
are trying to awaken.[8]

Ecuador's sole delegate, the aristocratic Enrique Dorn y
de Alsua, was another representative already in place when
the Conference finally began on 18 January. Paris had been
his home for many years. At the start Ecuador probably had
the lowest profile of the four Spanish-speaking South American countries at the Conference, yet in diplomatic terms all
four countries were in the same boat. If the others were to be
invited, then Ecuador had to be too. Ecuador's low profile
may help explain the confusion apparent in British diplomatic circles about just which of the South American countries had been invited to the Conference. For example, on 22
January – a full four days after the Conference was formally
opened – a British representative in Quito telegraphed British
officials at the Peace Conference in Paris to say that *if* the
Ecuadorians were to be invited to the Conference, it would
be provisionally represented by its current minister to London
and Paris, Dorn. A few days later a British official scribbled a
note underneath a copy of this telegraph saying that: 'I don't
imagine that Ecuador will be invited as the lists are now full.'
However, the official was clearly unaware – as possibly were
some diplomats in Quito – that Dorn was not only at the
Conference but that by this time he had already attended two
meetings. This had to be pointed out in a hand-written note
by another British official on the same document two days
later. 'The Ecuadorian Minister here has represented his government at both the Plenary Sessions which have so far taken
place, that State being among those which have broken off
diplomatic relations with the enemy Powers … '.[9]

However, although Ecuador had been admitted to the gathering it was not guaranteed a warm welcome by everyone. The bondholders who had invested in Ecuador's beleaguered Guayaquil and Quito Railway were still deeply unhappy that they had received little of the money they were owed. Now they saw a chance to act. As the Conference gathered they wrote to Lord Curzon at the Foreign Office in London wanting to know whether their grievances could be raised with the Ecuadorian delegation. This letter was passed on to former British prime minister and then foreign secretary Arthur Balfour on 3 February 1919. A more strongly-worded letter was to follow on the same subject in April. The bondholders' case was also supported by the Foreign Office's man in Quito, who said that when it came to the question of the payment of the railway debts he did 'not attach much importance to the promises of the Ecuadorian government'. British impatience with Ecuador came to a head when Dorn suggested his country had *taken an active part in the war and suffered losses thereby*. 'Ecuador suffered some loss of foreign trade, particularly in the matter of cacao exports,' conceded a British official. But he added that Ecuador 'would have been no better off if she had remained neutral'. And then for good measure he concluded: 'The government have defaulted in their payments to their foreign bondholders and are now touting for a loan that no one will advance without some sort of financial control.' [10]

Ecuador's diplomatic and economic 'baggage' was one further reason why it had little chance to make a mark on the proceedings of the Conference. However, few if any of the smaller nations had much hope of playing a major role as they were almost entirely irrelevant to Conference proceedings. The Great Powers – essentially the US, France and

Britain, with Italy and Japan playing walk-on, walk-off roles – had their own agendas, which they were determined to steamroller through. This agenda largely concerned the fate of Germany and the extent to which it should be made to pay for starting – and losing – the war, an issue with which France in particular was almost obsessed. Juan Buero, Uruguay's delegate, was acutely aware that he and his colleagues were far from centre-stage in Paris. 'The action of the Latin American delegates was very limited, the scene was absorbed by the European and U.S. delegates,' said his son.[11] The other major substantive issue dealt with in the preparation of the Treaty of Versailles was the establishment of the League of Nations, Woodrow Wilson's pet cause. Only on this issue could the South American nations even hope to have their voices heard.

Yet the South American delegates were nonetheless determined to make their presence felt at the Conference as best they could. Dorn was certainly not overawed by the idea of dealing with the political superpowers who sought to control the Conference. For one thing, he had already attended large gatherings, for example the 1907 Hague Conference, where there had been considerable diplomatic sniping between the US and Latin American nations. Dorn also felt at ease in his Paris surroundings and with his French hosts, doubtless far more so than some of the other delegates who had rarely visited the city. The wealthy diplomat also lived in some comfort; at one time the Ecuadorian's address was number 9, rue de la Bienfaisance, a fine house in the 8th arrondissement, once occupied by a French government minister. This did not, though, stop him complaining to Quito about the rising cost of everyday items in Paris during the Conference. *Just to give you some examples, a pair of boots that before the war were worth 45 francs now cost 150 … meals that you could have got for 5 francs you can't now find for 15 francs*, he informed his bosses.[12]

In addition to his comfortable lifestyle, the aristocratic Dorn also made some very influential friends. One of the most important of these was the celebrated Frenchman Baron Pierre de Coubertin, best known as the man behind the modern Olympic Games. Dorn and de Coubertin were both cultured men of a similar generation, and by the First World War the pair had become friends. The two men even helped create a debating contest known as the Coubertin Debate in Guayaquil, the first of which was held in May 1918.

With such powerful friends and contacts, it was perhaps not surprising that it was Dorn, along with the Brazilian head delegate Epitácio Pessoa, who felt comfortable in leading a mini 'revolt' of smaller countries over their representation on various commissions established by the Peace Conference. The organisation of the Conference was a complicated affair. In theory the main and most powerful body was the Plenary Conference, at which all countries designated on the Allied side were represented. However, this large, cumbersome body met infrequently and was essentially there to rubber-stamp decisions already made elsewhere. The real power lay with the Great Powers who ran what was in effect a cabinet office, the Bureau of the Conference. Alongside these bodies a series of commissions were established. These dealt with a range of specific issues, from those that arose directly from the war – such as war crimes – to those looking ahead to wider concerns, such as the commission on international labour legislation. Membership of these commissions was dominated by delegates from the major nations. But the smaller countries wanted their say, too, and a meeting of Powers with Special

Interests – the smaller nations – was created to decide how they should be represented on the commissions.

The first of these meetings was held on 27 January 1919 and was chaired by the French diplomat Jules Cambon. Its aim was to work out the representation of these smaller powers on four commissions; those dealing with the League of Nations, ports, international labour legislation and war crimes. However, the meeting had no power to decide how many of them should be on each commission, as this had already been decided by the Great Powers. The leading Allied countries would have ten delegates on each body, the smaller powers just five. Cambon's role was simply to help the smaller powers agree which of them would sit on which commission. The first meeting, conducted in French, took place in a calm and constructive atmosphere and eventually the smaller nations present – which included Ecuador, Peru, Bolivia and Uruguay – agreed to vote among themselves on how to carve up the commission slots. But already there were the first rumblings of discontent among the representatives about their lack of say. In particular, the Brazilian delega-tion was unhappy that membership of the commission on the League of Nations – the one issue that clearly affected all countries – was being restricted in this way. The Brazil-ian delegate João Pandiá Calógeras told Cambon that the principle of the League had already been agreed, and that it should be on the basis of one country, one vote. 'That is the spirit in which I beg leave to bring to your attention the argu-ments which appear to mitigate in favour of an increase in the number of members of Commissions, for the phrase "League of Nations" must not merely appear in our speeches; its spirit must live in our hearts,' he said.[13]

Though the smaller powers accepted at this January

meeting that they could not amend the number of commission members, *Calógeras* and others had fired a warning shot across the Great Powers' bows. Later, when the League of Nations Commission actually met, there was a revolt among the lesser powers, who succeeded in getting their representation increased from five to nine, though the only South American representative remained Brazil. The January meeting showed that the Latin American nations at the Peace Conference were co-operating in a way they rarely did back home. When potential places came up on some of the less contentious commissions, there was nearly always agreement on a candidate from the Americas. So when the Belgian delegate told the chairman that the powers had agreed on candidates for the Commission on International Legislation on Labour, he put forward the names 'Belgium, Serbia, Cuba for the South American [*sic*] group, Poland and the Czechoslovak Republic'. Uruguay was voted onto the Commission on the International Control of Ports, Waterways and Railways.[14]

By the time of a later meeting of the Powers with Special Interests on 3 March, the mood among the smaller nations had hardened considerably. The purpose of this gathering was to discuss membership of the Economic and Financial Commissions. As soon as it started the head of the Brazilian delegation, Epitácio Pessoa, revealed that the smaller nations had met informally in advance and reached a common position. This was to ask that their membership on these two commissions be increased from five to ten. It would be 'impossible' otherwise for them to 'satisfy the just requirements of their situation', said Pessoa, who in April would be elected president of his country. He therefore tabled a resolution urging Cambon to ask the Great Powers to reconsider their decision on membership numbers. The Frenchman was, however, reluctant to follow Pessoa's suggestions and the limitations of the smaller powers' 'bloc' became evident. Both the Greek and Belgian delegates agreed to back the chairman's compromise suggestion that the smaller nations vote for their five commission members – and also supply a list of extra names just in case the Great Powers saw fit to extend their representation. Nonetheless there was a widespread feeling among the countries present that the real Conference was taking place elsewhere behind closed doors and that they were being left out in the cold. Dorn, for example told Cambon that *members of the Conference should be kept informed of the labours of all the Commissions* and hoped that the *proofs of Minutes of the Commissions might be communicated to the Conference.*[15]

In the end the smaller powers agreed to vote on a list of ten representatives for each of the two commissions being discussed, reserving themselves the right to trim this number back to five if the Great Powers failed to extend membership from five to ten. This was a small but significant difference from the approach favoured by Cambon. Frustrated at their lack of influence in Paris, the smaller countries had thrown down the gauntlet to leaders such as Clemenceau, Lloyd George and Wilson. The South American countries played a prominent role in this mini act of defiance. Bolivia, Peru and Brazil were chosen as candidates for the Economics Commission, and Ecuador and Brazil for the Financial Commission. However, Uruguay – whose delegates Buero, Blanco and Acevedo were not at the meeting – appeared on neither list.

If the Paris minnows expected the bigger countries to give way on this question of commission representation, they were to be bitterly disappointed. The Supreme Allied Council (made up of the US, France, Britain, Italy and Japan) quickly dismissed the question of the commissions' make-up and insisted once again that the Powers with Special Interests be restricted to just five members on each. On 6 March the smaller nations met once more, this time to whittle their list of chosen representatives down from ten to five. It was now the cracks began to appear not just between the smaller countries and the dominating nations, but within the ranks of the smaller nations themselves. This split was caused by the fact that the Latin American nations were now clearly operating as a bloc within a bloc. The 'ringleaders' were said to be Pessoa from Brazil and Ecuador's Dorn. As a Greek delegate put it, during attempts to agree on the commission membership, the smaller powers had come up against a 'tendency on the part of the Latin American Powers to acquire more seats than they could obtain through an objective distribution which took European interests likewise into account'. Out of the five nations voted as candidates for the Financial Commission four – Peru, Brazil, Bolivia and Panama (in order of the number of votes received) – came from Latin America. The Greek delegate said it was 'shocking' that with the exception of Portugal all the countries that had taken the 'most active' part in the war had been eliminated from the list. He might have added that two of those voted in – Bolivia and Peru – had not even been at war. Latin American countries did almost equally well when the smaller nations voted for their candidates for the Economics Commission. Brazil came top, followed by China, Cuba, Siam (Thailand) and Ecuador. Not a single European state was on the list.[16]

The exasperated Greeks persuaded other European countries to abstain from voting on a supplementary 'reserve' list of countries. This was to be sent to the Supreme Council in case that body changed its mind and allowed more than five representatives from the smaller countries. Ironically, Greece featured on both reserve lists, as did Belgium. But the rift was clear. What had started out as a noble attempt by the smaller nations to make the Supreme Council take notice of them had descended into a rather less noble split between the continents. Countries such as Belgium – which all agreed had suffered horribly in the war – were to have no one on either the Financial or Economic Commission. Thanks to continental solidarity – and backing from Siam and China – the main beneficiaries of this mini power struggle appear to have been Peru, Ecuador and Bolivia. Ismael Montes and Dorn, who were present at all these meetings, appeared to have won something of a diplomatic coup not just for their own countries but for their neighbour too.

Any joy they may have felt at this 'victory' was short-lived, however. The members of the Supreme Council were adamant that they were not going to have two potentially important commissions full of delegates from nations whose very presence at the Paris Peace Conference had been in doubt until the last minute. Sensitive to the complaints about a lack of representation, the Great Powers did enlarge the number of seats for the smaller nations – to six from five on the Financial Commission and from five to seven on the Economic Commission. But they completely changed the commission memberships, booting out the Latin American delegates and replacing them with representatives from European countries. Brazil, a close ally of the US, was the only Latin American country retained from the list and was given a place on the Economic Commission. Ecuador, Bolivia and Peru were all removed.

The Latin American nations were outraged. Indeed they were so angry that at a series of impromptu Latin American 'bloc' meetings there was talk of walking out of the Conference over what was seen as a very clear insult. In fact, there was more than just talk about walking out. Extraordinary though it may seem, the American delegation believed that some of these angry countries were preparing to do the unthinkable – talk directly to the enemy themselves. In an anxious memorandum to President Wilson, Secretary of State Lansing and other members of the American delegation warned that some of the South American delegates have ' ... gone so far as to say that they should ... possibly try to make a separate peace with Germany'. It was an astonishing threat. Of course, the idea that Ecuador, Bolivia, Peru and others would go off and negotiate with the Germans – a state against which they had not even been at war – was close to inconceivable. Nonetheless, the mere fact that it was being mooted highlights the depth of anger felt by these countries. Arguably even more damaging for President Wilson, there was also a threat to the American leader's pet project for the Conference – the League of Nations. As Lansing warned his boss: 'There were also remarks made to the effect that if such an action as this on the part of the powerful nations was to be an indication of what the Great Powers would do in the League of Nations, it was best for them not to enter the League.' Of course, the Latin American delegates knew their audience; they were certainly very aware how much the League meant to Wilson and calculated that this threat alone would get his attention. After all, what would it say about 'his' League if it started life by being boycotted by nations from America's own backyard?[17]

The Americans were certainly worried. Lansing wrote of the 'very hard feelings against the Great Powers', even using the word 'crisis' to describe the situation. He was particularly worried that the row might allow German propaganda 'which is only dormant in South and Central America' to gain a hold and undermine the work of the Conference. Another concern was the risk of the US's relations with its neighbours being 'seriously impaired' by the affair. However, Lansing and his team also understood that the main issue of concern for countries such as Ecuador, Bolivia and Peru was not membership of the Financial and Economic Commissions *per se* but one of national 'pride'. With the aid of careful diplomacy, the US delegation helped quell the simmering Latin American indignation. The threat to quit the Conference and talk to Germany direct had, after all, been a 'diplomatic threat' – one intended to make sure the other side (in this case the Great Powers) took notice of their complaint.[18]

Another reason why countries such as Ecuador, Bolivia and Peru were most unlikely ever to carry through their threats to quit the Conference was that they had other diplomatic goals to achieve and too much to lose. Peru and Bolivia, for example, hoped the Conference might solve their Pacific coast dispute with Chile. Moreover, frustrated as they were at being ignored or rebuffed by the Great Powers, the four South American nations were consoled by the fact that they were at least present at the biggest diplomatic gathering in the world, while neighbours back home – Chile, Argentina, Colombia and Paraguay – were not. It was their big chance to be seen on the world stage, to stand alongside the United States and its President Woodrow Wilson, and to raise their own national issues as best they could. For all these countries, just being in Paris was a kind of diplomatic triumph.

5
The Treaty of Versailles and its Outcome 1919

One fringe benefit for the delegates from the three Andean countries and Uruguay was that the Conference gave them a unique insight into European politics and decisions that were to shape the world for the coming decades. They were also shrewd enough to spot some of the future problems that were being stored up even as the Conference delegates wrestled to deal with the peace terms.

Ismael Montes, for one, proved that he was a thoughtful observer of the negotiations from his Paris vantage point. The veteran politician watched with increasing concern at the way the Allies treated defeated Germany, with France leading the way in its desire to ensure that its neighbour could no longer pose a military threat, and was worried that Allied demands for war reparations were in danger of going too far. He felt that the victors' position had shifted since the start of the Conference to one that now exhibited a *complete extinction of generous feelings*. He added: *The Allies now talk of nothing but the complete payment of their expenditure and full reparation for damages caused. The idea that now dominates public opinion is that [Germany] must now pay everything, absolutely everything, even if that exceeds the limits of what is humanly possible.* The outcome of this approach, in Montes' view, was that the deep well of sympathy that the Allies, and in particular France, had from other countries was now in danger of being dissipated. *The main objective of the Allies in respect to Germany is to reduce it to military impotence and all their efforts are channelled to that end; but they exaggerate the matter so much that sympathy is beginning to slip away [from them]. It seems that the friends of the Entente accompany them with less enthusiasm in victory than they did in war,* said the Bolivian. Most worryingly of all Montes saw, prophetically as it turned out, that the Allies' approach was creating problems for the future. In an acute piece of observation he told his diplomatic masters: *The Peace is not yet signed and one can already see the seeds of a new war. The hatred that is mounting up in the defeated [nations] may well be stronger than all the measures being taken to crush them. Germany will recover, despite all the efforts being taken to keep her down, and when it feels strong again, the virtues of the race will surely put them back in the front rank [of nations].*[1]

Montes also realised that the Great Powers were not always speaking with one voice, certainly not behind closed doors. He noted that Britain and the United States had a different approach to the German question from the French. *It is apparent that Britain and the US are keen to re-open economic relations with Germany – this is the subject of some jealousy on the part of the French and Italians. It seems the*

> **'The Peace is not yet signed and one can already see the seeds of a new war.'**
> ISMAEL MONTES

Americans and British are keen to combat Russian Bolshevism in this way, as well as, naturally enough, stimulate their own economic activities, he wrote. Most of all, though, he spotted a divergence between the stance of Woodrow Wilson and that of Britain and France over German indemnities to the Allies. In April, as the question of how much Germany should pay and to whom came to a head, Montes considered that Wilson's proposals were not acceptable to Britain and especially France. *As a result of this, Wilson, yesterday's saviour, is today blamed for the failure of the peace, and as a consequence he is the subject of harsh criticism. He is seen as an ideologue, a dreamer, a Germanophile,* wrote the former Bolivian president. The Uruguayan delegate Juan Carlos Blanco could also see the cracks in the Allied side, including those between Britain and France. He wrote that there was considerable resentment in France against Britain – or 'England' as he called it – in general and its Prime Minister Lloyd George in particular. The reason, Blanco, told his bosses in Montevideo, was that immediately after the November Armistice Britain had been 'inflexible' in its desire to see removed all German infrastructure and equipment – coastal artillery maritime defence, military and civilian fleets – that could threaten it and its colonies in the future. Yet later, when faced with France's own demands against Germany, Britain changed its tone and expressed concern about not provoking the enemy and risk 'throwing her into the arms of the Bolsheviks', said Blanco. 'M. Clemenceau fought against this reasoning with great tenacity,' he concluded.[2]

The Uruguayans clearly had time for the old 'tiger' Clemenceau, a man who unlike most senior delegates at the talks had actually been to Uruguay. Blanco, for example, seemed to relish the old man's famed stubbornness and passion for his cause, describing the French premier's feats as 'remark-able'. While Lloyd George's main preoccupation seemed to be to try to maintain his country's friendship with the United States, Clemenceau had managed to obtain some positive achievements for France by 'handling every subject with an obstinacy and firmness before which Messieurs Wilson and Lloyd George generously gave way on more than one occa-sion'. Meanwhile, Blanco noted that delegates 'from all the other countries' were subordinate to these three men, even those from Italy and Japan. Perhaps a smaller state such as Uruguay could not help but find some comfort in seeing that they were not alone in being excluded from the very top table at Paris. It may have been a message that Montevideo wanted to hear.[3]

Given the Uruguay delegation's clear fondness for Clem-enceau, it is hardly surprising that its members were shocked when news came through that the Frenchman had been shot during the Conference. The attack happened on 19 February as the veteran politician left his home to attend a meeting with President Wilson's adviser Colonel House and the British foreign secretary Arthur Balfour. The would-be assassin leapt out and fired seven shots at the car in which Clemenceau was sitting. Fortunately for him just one hit the target, and even this bullet managed to miss all his vital organs. Clemenceau was thus able to be up and walking within a day and back at work within a week. But though he publicly shrugged off the shooting – he lamented the poor marksmanship of his French assailant, for example – the attack shook both him and world opinion. The spectre of communism – some ini-tially thought that this might have been a Bolshevik-inspired attack – was already hanging over the Conference after the Russian Revolution. Many feared that Germany, destabilised by the war defeat, could itself succumb to Bolshevism. The attack on Clemenceau made the threat of political radicalism and violence seem very real to the Peace Conference delegates in Paris.

The representatives from the various Latin American delegations joined together to send a telegram to Clemenceau's house. As well as indicating their genuine sense of shock, the joint communication also underlined the extent to which the Latin American delegates operated as a bloc on occasions. The telegram on 20 February expressed their nations' 'profound sympathy' and their 'indignation' at the attempt on his life, and wished the French premier a 'quick and complete recovery'. It was signed by Montes for Bolivia, Dorn for Ecuador, García Calderón for Peru and Blanco for Uruguay, as well as by other Latin American delegates. A reply to the delegates made on Clemenceau's behalf suggests that the politician was genuinely touched by this gesture. 'I ask you to communicate to all the Latin American representatives his feelings of deep gratitude,' said the reply. A week later Blanco was writing to the foreign ministry in Montevideo full of admiration for Clemenceau, and noting the impact of the assassination attack on public opinion in France. 'The attack against M. Clemenceau has increased even more the popularity of this great man,' he wrote. Even though he had been hit by a bullet, this had 'not reduced the energy of M [sic] Clemenceau who can count on the support of all sections of French society apart from the extreme socialists'.[4]

The frustration of the Latin American nations at their inability to influence events did not disappear as the Conference continued; indeed in some ways it increased as spring arrived, and as attention switched away from the League and focused even more on the German question. It led to suspicion among some of the smaller powers that they were being deliberately kept out of the loop about what was going on. The irritation felt by the Uruguayan delegation, for example, was expressed in a letter Blanco sent to Lloyd George and the heads of the French, American and Italian delegations on 19 April. The tone is wounded rather than angry, but even though couched in polite diplomatic terms, the Uruguayan's meaning is clear. Blanco begins by pointing out that Uruguay had not been invited to a recent meeting that had taken place at the Ministry of Foreign Affairs in Paris. He then makes it clear that, despite this, the delegation 'wishes to be able to follow, like the other nations taking part in the Conference, the preliminaries of the peace with Germany'. Blanco then rehearses the by now familiar litany of what his country had done for the Allied war effort, including the carrying out of patrols to help secure Allied commercial shipping. It therefore 'seemed necessary' that information about the peace negotiations should be given to Uruguay's delegates in good time, in other words 'at the same time as other nations invited to the Peace Conference'. However, what really seems to have hurt Blanco and the rest of the Uruguayan delegation is that some of those 'other nations' who they felt were getting information before them were countries who had 'not participated in any way' in the war. They had been invited simply because they had 'declared hostilities' against Germany. Though Blanco does not refer to anyone by name, he appears to be writing about some of the small Central American countries who, although they had declared war in line with the US, had contributed little or nothing to the war effort itself. If so, then it shows the limitations of Latin American solidarity at the Conference. Blanco ends by stating that the delegation 'dares to hope' that, through the help of Lloyd George, Uruguay will be 'called to take part in decisions and deliberations' in common with other countries. The letter was answered by Balfour, who was clearly baffled as to why the Uruguayans were so unhappy. As his reply makes clear, Balfour had no idea to what meeting Blanco was referring and thus from what the Uruguayans felt excluded.[5]

In fact, the Uruguayans had more reason to feel engaged in the Peace Conference than their fellow Spanish-speaking South American nations represented in Paris. While Peru, Bolivia and Ecuador had been left with no say on the Financial and Economic Commissions, after the overruling by the Great Powers, Uruguay remained on the Commission on the International Control of Ports, Waterways and Railways. As a maritime country, Uruguay had been a logical choice to be on this commission, and Blanco was the man chosen to represent it.

Despite the frustrations, Buero was still enjoying the experience. The fact that he was in the city of his birth witnessing a great moment in history was enough reason alone for him to relish it. But that was not the end of the good news. The young politician and diplomat had already risen quickly in his short career. On 1 March Buero went a step further when he was appointed Foreign Minister by Baltasar Brum, the new president. Buero was not asked to return from Paris to take up his duties immediately. Doubtless reasoning that Buero was likely to have more useful contact with world leaders at the Peace Conference than back in Montevideo, Brum appointed Daniel Munoz as acting foreign minister until the young diplomat's return.

The following month, Buero had yet more reasons to be feeling good about life. One of the very few occasions on which a smaller state had a chance to make its presence felt was during the infrequent Plenary Sessions. At the session on 28 April Juan Antonio Buero made a short speech, in which he outlined his country's commitment to international co-operation. The confident and eloquent Buero had always been noted as a public speaker and his words now struck home with the most powerful man present – President Woodrow Wilson. Later Wilson sent the young Uruguayan a private note in which he wrote: 'Your statement was admirable. I fully recognize the leadership Uruguay has shown in all liberal reform and in the international co-operation for peace.' He signed the note 'WW'. In her diary kept during the Conference, Mrs Wilson's social secretary Edith Benham shed more light on Wilson's views on both Buero and Uruguay. 'The delegate from Uruguay made an excellent and very short speech. The P[resident] in commenting on it tonight said that Uruguay in its legislation and laws is the most advanced country in the world and he said he wrote a little note to the delegate complimenting him on what he said which bore out the reputation his country enjoyed.' Buero was delighted to receive the American president's note and it has remained in his family's keeping, where it is still a considerable source of pride.[6]

Buero's good standing with the US delegation at the Conference and his new status as Foreign Minister-in-waiting also allowed him to engage in discussions that were not strictly part of the Conference agenda. This included talks about Uruguay signing a bilateral arbitration treaty with the United States. Before the start of the war the then US Secretary of State, William Jennings Bryan, had been a strong advocate of such agreements. Somewhat naively perhaps, he believed that using arbitration panels and having 'cooling off' periods in disputes would help prevent war. Wilson was also a fan of these agreements. Now during the Conference, US Secretary of State Robert Lansing and Buero discussed the outline of an agreement. In a telegram on 19 June, Buero asked for *urgent instructions* about how to proceed. There were two reasons for his haste. One was that President Wilson was still in Paris at the time. Once he left, Buero warned that it would be *impossible* to negotiate the treaty further, because of all the other various legal and political problems that the President would have to handle later when he returned to the United States. Secondly, there was the prestige that it would bring. *Uruguay would thus be the first country to sign an extended arbitration agreement with the United States.* However, Montevideo did not share Buero's need for speed and the advice he received was far from decisive.[7]

> ' ... Absolute destruction ... systematic destruction carried out by Germans in 1917 in places where there was no fighting.'
>
> JUAN BUERO

As a break from the endless discussions and meetings, Buero was anxious to see at first hand the damage caused by the bloody struggle. In common with other Latin American delegates – for example Epitácio Pessoa of Brazil – he felt that witnessing the destruction would bring home to him the huge importance of what they were discussing at the Conference. Accordingly, he and other members of the Uruguayan team left their comfortable rooms in Paris and travelled to Louvain in Belgium. It was here that German troops had looted and burnt buildings for five days in late August 1914, prompting some of the earliest international headlines about German wartime atrocities.

The same delegation also visited Ypres, scene of some of the worst fighting in the war. Buero and his companions were clearly moved by the sights of *absolute destruction* they witnessed. He was also struck by the sheer ferocity of the German actions. *Systematic destruction carried out by Germans in 1917 in places where there was no fighting*, he telegraphed Montevideo. But the three-day visit to Belgium also had its less grim side for the visitor. He and the rest of his team were feted by the Belgians and treated to a banquet in their honour, having had *very cordial* talks with government ministers. Buero, toasting his hosts' royal family, passed on his own and his country's best wishes for Belgium's future *prosperity* and praised the way the country had coped with its tribulations with *dignity and steadfastness*. There was also business to discuss; Uruguayan and Belgian representatives were keen to boost trade links between the two countries. During the trip King Albert decorated Buero with the Belgian Grand Cross in honour both of him and his country.[8]

One of the few live issues that was directly relevant to the South American nations during the Conference was that of shipping; either merchant vessels lost to German attacks or German shipping detained in ports by the countries involved. This particularly applied to Peru, which lost the *Lorton* in 1917 to a German submarine and which also seized a number of ships, and also to Uruguay, which claimed the loss of two vessels – the *Gorizia* and the *Rosario* – and had also seized German ships in its ports. For Brazil, which had taken control of a number of enemy ships, the issue became a major source of tension at the Conference – nations such as Britain considering it rather less worthy of consideration than losses among the main combatants. But for Uruguay and Peru the fate of this shipping and the extent to which they should be compensated did not become major issues. These questions were in fact ultimately submitted to the maritime service of the Reparations Commission after the Conference and dealt with later, in 1920 and 1921.

The South American delegates all kept busy in Paris, and attended rounds of social engagements as well as diplomatic meetings. But they were still rarely able to penetrate the big discussions, let alone influence them. Indeed, had most of the South American delegates not already been based in Europe, they might well have wondered about the usefulness of the time they spent in Paris between January and June 1919. But they did not stop trying to get more involved. In late March Ecuador's Dorn y de Alsua was still piqued about his country's lack of representation on any of the Conference commissions, and especially the economic and financial ones. In a letter to the Conference organisers the Ecuadorian delegation complained

BRAZIL'S ROLE AT PARIS
Brazil was the only South American country to declare war on Germany, and because of that and its size and strategic importance to the US, it was allowed three delegates at the Peace Conference – two more than any other Latin American country. The leader of its delegation Epitácio Pessoa – who was elected Brazilian president during his time in Paris – helped organise a bloc of smaller powers at the Conference and also one of the Latin American countries. Brazil's chief ally in Paris was the US – the British delegation, for example, were irritated by the South American country's dogged and narrow focus on its own financial interests.

that the exclusion of countries such as Ecuador from the membership lists *had no other impact than to exclude from [those commissions] countries that had taken an effective part in the war and suffered damages as a result.* The letter, which was unsigned but was in French and almost certainly written by the French-speaking Dorn, continued in similar tone: *The Economic Commission was of general interest to countries and it seems that this was the occasion in which to admit into its ranks the representatives of countries that had not hesitated to compromise their economic future by ranging themselves on the side of the Allies.* The note ended by suggesting that it was *regrettable* that the initial vote of the smaller nations had been overturned by the Great Powers when *surely a more friendly solution could have been reached.*

'The elegant battles of the past have given way to obscure pain and underground heroism.'
FRANCISCO GARCÍA CALDERÓN

Dorn's note had no impact, however; this is hardly surprising given the British delegation's rather jaundiced view of Ecuador's war suffering.[9]

The senior Peruvian delegate Francisco Garcia Calderón was also busy, both as his country's official representative in Belgium and as a representative at the Conference. That however did not stop the prolific writer from producing a 290-page book devoted to the war that he managed to complete in June 1919, around the time the Treaty was signed. Titled *El Dilema de la Gran Guerra* ('The Dilemma of the Great War)', this was no mere journalistic assessment of the politics and military aspects of the war and its aftermath, but instead a lengthy philosophical treatise on the nature of war and its meaning in contemporary times, economically, politically and socially. The book is eloquent about the horrors of the uniquely bloody trench warfare that had just taken place. *The elegant battles of the past have given way to obscure pain and underground heroism*, writes García Calderón, painfully aware of his own brother's death on those killing fields. The following pages are full of literary and historical references including Hegel, Darwin, Genghis Khan, John Stuart Mill, de Tocqueville, Bismarck and a host of other great thinkers and historical figures. Much of the work was far more wide-ranging and theoretical than the more narrowly focused discussions around the Conference. García Calderón did, however, use the opportunity to single out Paris – the venue for the Conference and the city he had chosen to make his home for many years – for special praise. This was the *capital of the West* that joined together the *might of the French* with the *hopes of the liberal world*. This was why early in the war the Germans had sought to march on Paris – almost as a kind of tribute to its importance. *This march of the dark legions was a bloody homage to invincible civilisation*. Paris, said García Calderón, had been converted into a fortress – a *fortress of reason*, and a city that *would never die*. It would certainly have made good reading for his French hosts.[10]

The rather less literary Montes was also busy writing. In his case, however, the works in question were lengthy memorandums home on the issues being discussed at Paris and in particular the issue that most concerned Bolivia. This was regaining access to the Pacific Ocean. Tacna and Arica were subjects never far from Montes' pen and lips during the Conference and he had his own hard-headed and practical approach. He insisted, for example, that his country's proposals on the issue should be detailed and tangible rather than dealing in generalities, otherwise nobody would take them seriously. *When dealing with Peru – who won't have a problem in agreeing with us – they will point us in the direction of Chile. And when we speak to Chile, they will point us in the direction of Peru. So it's vital to keep this discussion a concrete one*, he wrote. The former president wrote freely, in the manner of someone who, as he suggested, had retired from domestic politics. Having no urge to *criticise over the affair*, he simply wanted to ensure that the Foreign Ministry in La Paz stayed focused on its policy on the Tacna and Arica disputes and did not get side-tracked or change tactic. *It's not a case of all roads lead to Rome. If you take the wrong one, you will fail*. And he hinted that he would quit foreign affairs altogether if this issue simply became a matter of political party squabbling back home.[11]

Peru and Bolivia both raised the issue of Tacna and Arica before and during the Conference. But the Great Powers were anxious not to get waylaid by such disputes. It was not that the US or Britain felt that the Tacna and Arica dispute was unimportant. Both had their own trade and strategic interests in the region and were keen to see an end to the long-running affair. It was more a question of keeping the Conference and its delegates on the main task in hand: laying down the blueprint for peace in Europe. The extent to which British delegates became irritated – even with their own countrymen – over non-core issues being raised is shown by their reaction to a Foreign Office memorandum. The document, which was sent to the British delegation in Paris, detailed Bolivia's ongoing complaints about British trade and financial restrictions at the end of the war. At the bottom, an exasperated British official in Paris has written: 'I do not understand why the FO sent us this correspondence.' In the end the issue was left to be dealt with by the new League of Nations.[12]

Though they were mostly on the sidelines of events, this did not stop the South American delegations from getting swept up in the mood of tension and excitement as the day approached for the signing of the Treaty of Versailles. Almost until the last minute there was suspense over whether Germany would sign a peace treaty it clearly felt was both deeply unfair and humiliating. On 23 June, the day when the deadline given for the response from Berlin expired, word came through that Germany had finally decided to put its name to the document. There was relief and jubilation, not just among the delegates, but back home too. 'The Peace Treaty signing will take place before Friday,' announced *El*

Diario in Montevideo, a little prematurely as it turned out. The signing was later set for Saturday 28 June. *El Diario* also reported the jubilation among the French at news of the decision, and the fact that President Wilson would be returning home to the United States immediately after the signing. But more ominously it also commented on the depth of German unhappiness at the terms of the peace treaty.

The South American delegates also had mixed feelings. There was relief that the long and often fruitless months of negotiations were over. But Ismael Montes was hardly alone in his feelings of foreboding. During the negotiations, as the shape of the final treaty began to emerge, the veteran politician had been worried that representatives from the victorious powers had been more concerned with *vengeance* than with *justice*. Little had occurred in the subsequent weeks to change his mind.[13]

Yet the dominant mood was one of excitement; it was after all a chance to take part in a true historical drama, an opportunity that comes but rarely in political and diplomatic life. Juan Buero, for one, was very aware of the momentous nature of the event. *Finally the sacred day of the signature arrived, Saturday 28 June 1919*, Buero later told his son. *Paris was covered with flags and the joy was immense.* The delegates gathered in the Hall of Mirrors at the Palace of Versailles, a place where, Buero said, *history was waiting.* The delegates began arriving in the afternoon and Buero had a close-up view of the dramatic moment when the German representatives entered the hall. *The German Delegates – Mr Hermann Muller and Mr [Johannes] Bell followed by their secretaries arrived at quarter past three and sat down between the Uruguayan and Japanese delegation.* After the Germans had signed the Treaty, it was the turn of all the delegates to sign, going up in alphabetical order once the representatives of the Great Powers had signed. This meant Bolivia's Ismael Montes was the first Latin American delegate to sign. A number of delegates used the lull of the signing to get their programmes signed by other delegates as a memento of the day; according to one report, Montes was the first to approach the two German representatives, who had hitherto sat, ignored, on their own. Dorn of Ecuador came next among the Spanish-speaking South American nations, followed by Candamo for Peru. Each of these lesser powers were only allowed one official delegate at a time to the Conference, so as Peruvian minister in France he signed rather than García Calderón, who was now minister in Belgium. Finally, at five minutes to four, the final delegate stepped forward to sign, Buero from Uruguay. After a flourish from the young politician's pen the ceremony was declared formally over – the Treaty of Versailles had been signed.[14]

'... A new period of history for the whole of humanity.'
ENRIQUE DORN Y DE ALSUA

There were parties in Paris at which the delegates could toast the signing of this historic treaty and celebrations, too, back in South America, where diplomatic messages of congratulation were exchanged. Relaxing in the French capital Dorn took stock of what the event meant for a country such as Ecuador, summing up how many Latin Americans felt at the time. Writing three weeks later to the Foreign Ministry in Quito he said: *I congratulate our government for having worked in order that our country should be one of the participants in this solemn consecration of law, which without doubt heralds a new period of history for the whole of humanity. No doubt it will benefit Ecuador in time, in its dealing with the Allies, but meanwhile its affiliation is justified by disinterested motives that do honour to our country.*[15]

So finally, and after five months, the main work of the Conference was coming to a close. Though meetings and commissions continued, as far as Ecuador, Peru, Bolivia and Uruguay were concerned, the main issue had already been decided. Their gaze would soon turn to the one concrete achievement of the treaty negotiations that was likely to have a direct impact on their countries. This was the creation of the League of Nations.

Envoys of the American republics are photographed at the White House. They include, from the left, Costa Rica's Luis Fernandez, Honduran Julian Caceres, Ecuador's Colon Eloy Alfaro and Uruguay's Juan Carlos Blanco.

III

The Legacy

6

The League of Nations 1919–25

The creation of a League of Nations was Woodrow Wilson's great hope for the 1919 Paris Peace Conference. Though the idea for such an international body was not originally his, all ideas need a champion. And in the US president, the League found a very able and powerful champion indeed. Wilson gave a public declaration of the League's purpose when he addressed Congress on 8 January 1918. Wilson's speech was an ambitious attempt to set out a new policy for the world, a policy that was a response not just to the European war but also to the seizure of power in Russia by Lenin's Bolsheviks. The last of his Fourteen Points called for the establishment of a 'general association of nations' that would be able to afford 'mutual guarantees of political independence and territorial integrity to great and small states alike'. As we have already seen, countries such as Bolivia had drawn inspiration from parts of Wilson's speech to support their claims for access to the Pacific coast. Now Latin American nations as a whole saw that this new American-backed League of Nations, which Wilson was determined to create at the Paris Peace Conference, could also hold benefits for them.[1]

The Latin American view of the League of Nations, however, was different from that of the US and Wilson. For the American president it was a lofty attempt to resolve the world's disputes through the medium of one central organisation. But it was not intended to provide a check on America's freedom of action. For their part the South American countries, too, applauded the high-principled nature of the League, which generally chimed with their own declarations concerning freedom and self-determination. They also saw membership as a matter of prestige; to be part of the League of Nations was to be accepted at the top table of world diplomacy (even if they were likely to be seated at the bottom end of that table). But for these nations there was also another much more calculated reason for supporting the creation of the League of Nations. They saw the organisation as a potential counterbalance to the power of the United States in the region.

Before the war, there had been concern in South America about the growing power of the 'northern colossus' and what it might mean for them. American intervention in the Caribbean, Central America and Mexico merely served to exacerbate those fears. Was the United States interested in pan-American co-operation as it sometimes proclaimed? Or was it more interested in dominating the southern countries, intervening when and where it felt necessary? Even the principled Wilson – who had condemned US intervention in the region in the past – had found himself overtly trying to influence Mexican internal affairs, and sending the Marines into Haiti in 1915 to restore order, protect the approaches to the Panama Canal and ward off any potential German intervention.

'Against the policy of respect for Latin liberties are ranged the instincts of a triumphant plutocracy.'
FRANCISCO GARCÍA CALDERÓN

At the heart of Latin American concerns about US intentions was the application of the Monroe Doctrine. Initially seen – at least by Washington – as a way of ensuring that European nations were kept out of American affairs, the Doctrine had come to take on a different guise by the early 20th century.

Latin American countries disliked the Doctrine, believing its aim was not just to keep European nations out but also to justify Washington meddling in Latin American countries. Peru's Peace Conference delegate, Francisco García Calderón, had been a strong critic of the Monroe Doctrine before the war. He accepted that American intervention in Latin America had seen positive benefits – for example in helping to resolve conflicts between countries in the region. But he was critical of the way that the US now viewed its neighbours to the south. *The Monroe Doctrine has undergone an essential transformation; it has passed successively from the defensive to intervention and thence to the offensive.* García Calderón pointed out that during the course of the 19th and early 20th centuries the US had expanded – first into Louisiana and Florida, then into Texas, Mexico and Alaska. Hawaii followed, as did the Philippines, Puerto Rico and Guam. *Interventions have become more frequent*

THE MONROE DOCTRINE
The Monroe Doctrine, announced by American President James Monroe in 1823, aimed to deter European powers from interfering in North, Central and South America. It stated that any new interference in the region's nations by European countries would be treated as an aggressive act by the United States. This was a time when many South American states were fighting for independence. As American power grew stronger, though, many South American nations came to see the Doctrine as a justification for American intervention rather than something that protected them. Such fears grew In 1904 when President Theodore Roosevelt introduced the Roosevelt Corollary to the Doctrine, justifying United States intervention in Central America and the Caribbean in the name of economic stability.

with the expansion of frontiers, he warned. García Calderón believed that economic and financial interests were the main motivation for US intervention. *Against the policy of respect for Latin liberties are ranged the instincts of a triumphant plutocracy.*[2]

During the war such sentiments did not disappear but they were sometimes muted; South America needed the United States as an outlet for its goods and Washington was also the most likely protector from potential, if unlikely, German aggression. Afterwards, however, and as South and Central American countries began to realise just how dependent the war had made them on the US for trade, their concern re-emerged. For them the creation of the League of Nations created a golden opportunity for them to be a member of the same club as the US, and moreover a club in which all the members had to abide by the same rules. Under such an organisation, the territorial integrity of countries such as Bolivia and Ecuador would not just be protected from attack by their immediate neighbours – but against the US as well.

That at least was the thinking of Bolivia, Ecuador, Peru and Uruguay and other Latin American nations as they sent their delegations to Paris in 1919. Though none of the four nations had a representative on the League of Nations Commission in Paris, the region was represented by Brazil, whose chief delegate and future president Epitácio Pessoa showed he was to be no pushover. Co-operating with delegates from other smaller countries, Pessoa was one of the delegates who helped to increase the number of less powerful nations represented on the Commission, against the wishes of Wilson himself.

There was, however, an early setback for Latin American hopes over the likely ability of the League to protect them against Washington. By early 1919 it was already clear that Wilson faced severe domestic opposition back home over the new international body. For his critics, the idea that the US should sign up to a League which would shackle its freedom to act in its own backyard, while at the same time threatening to entangle the US in unnecessary foreign disputes, was anathema. Aware of the need to make concessions to his domestic opponents, Wilson therefore insisted that the League's Covenant made it clear that it did not conflict with – that is, override – the Monroe Doctrine. An initial attempt by Wilson to make this proviso part of Article 10 of the Covenant, which dealt with enforcement issues, was scuppered by the French. For them the League of Nations meant one thing and one thing only, namely the chance to call upon the help of powerful allies in the event of attack by its enemy Germany. If the League could not achieve this, then it was next to useless. They feared Wilson's insertion of this clause would give Washington a get-out clause should such an attack occur.

Eventually it was agreed that the Doctrine should be dealt with in its own article. Article 21 thus stated that nothing in the Covenant should be 'deemed to affect the validity of international engagements, such as ... the Monroe Doctrine, for securing the maintenance of peace'. Interestingly, there are no reports that the sole Latin American representative on the commission, Epitácio Pessoa of Brazil, raised any serious objections to the inclusion of this clause; the main opposition came from the French. The delegate from Honduras, who spoke at the Plenary Session that adopted the Covenant on 28 April, did complain publicly about the Monroe Doctrine clause. But as he spoke in Spanish and was understood by few at the meeting, his views were ignored. It certainly did not stop the Article being voted through.

The inclusion of such an article was, on the face of it, extraordinary. The Covenant was supposed to bind nations to behave according to its rules, but this left the US free to follow its own course wherever it felt the Monroe Doctrine applied. Thus, at one stroke, one of the main reasons why Latin American nations had felt reassured by the League of Nations was removed. What use was it signing up to the rules of a club, if its biggest member could follow its own, separate rules when it saw fit? The blanket of protection that Latin American nations hoped League membership would give them against Washington was now looking decidedly threadbare. Yet they had little choice but to accept the League of Nations as it was, Monroe Doctrine and all. For one thing, to stay out of the League would surely leave them even more vulnerable than they would be in joining it. Inside the body they would at least have an international platform to air grievances against the US. Secondly, they also had their own local issues that they wanted to put before the League once it was set up.

For Peru this meant Arica and Tacna, and for Bolivia this meant a gateway to the Pacific. Even before the League was established, the two Andean countries had seen the Paris Peace Conference as a venue for getting the disputes discussed. The fact that both these neighbouring countries were focused on the same stretch of coastline merely added to the complications, for them and for everyone else. For Peru it was essentially a bilateral matter between itself and Chile; for Bolivia it involved Chile and/or Peru, depending on where their longed-for outlet to the Pacific would be created. Both had hoped, and continued to hope, that the good offices of Washington might help them to resolve the dispute without involving more nations or multi-lateral organisations. But neither country wanted to miss out on the opportunity to bring the topic to the notice of the greatest gathering of world leaders and diplomats that had taken place for many years. Especially as Chile, whose neutrality had been steadfast throughout the war, was not going to get a formal place at the Conference table.

The question for the two nations was simply how a decades-old border dispute in South America could find its way onto the agenda of a Peace Conference whose main focus was the aftermath of a European war that had only just ended. As discussed in the previous chapter, the main powers, the United States, Britain and France, certainly did not want to get bogged down by a bilateral dispute between Chile and Peru. Bolivia's claims possibly represented a more complex matter – for the Americans, at least – as their claim to a legal right to a sea outlet was in theory backed by President Wilson's own Fourteen Points. But there were strong reasons why the US was very reluctant to let either issue be dealt with formally at the Conference, quite apart from the fact that these issues had nothing to do with the First World War. One was that Chile was an important and powerful country in the region, and the US had no desire to antagonise Santiago unnecessarily. Some in the State Department felt Chile would be at a disadvantage in relation to Peru and Bolivia, simply because it was not at the Conference. Another key reason was that Washington did not want Britain and other European countries getting involved in what they saw as an issue exclusively for the Americas. This, it was felt, would breach the Monroe Doctrine. Once again we see here a contradiction between American (especially Wilson's) support for the League of Nations and the desire of at least some elements in the US to ensure that its 'exclusive rights' to Latin America as implied in the Monroe Doctrine were maintained.

The solution for the Americans – as well as the Peruvians and the Bolivians – seemed to be to defer the issue of Tacna and Arica and Bolivian access to the sea to the League of Nations once that body was established. After all, as signatories to the Treaty of Versailles, Peru and Bolivia would become founder-members of the League. Meanwhile, there was also a move to invite neutral nations to take the steps necessary to join the League once the Treaty had been signed. To this end they were invited to Paris to discuss membership of the new body. Among the neutral countries invited to sign up for the Covenant were a number from Latin America, including Paraguay, Venezuela, Colombia, Argentina and Chile. For the founders of the League it was important that as many suitable countries join it as soon as possible to enhance its authority.

Chile, however, was less than enthusiastic about the idea of the Tacna and Arica dispute being dealt with by the League. Santiago felt it had the upper hand in the dispute, diplomatically and certainly militarily, and did not want to risk that advantage. It was now that Chile – at least according to the Bolivian interpretation – stalled for time, using its potential membership of the League as a bargaining chip. When President Wilson explored the possibility of sending the Tacna-Arica issue to the League to be considered, after the Covenant had been agreed in Paris on 28 April, the Chileans made it known to Washington that in the event of such a referral it would delay its entry into the League. At the same time, Santiago said it had its own plan to resolve this issue with a solution that would cede land to Peru as well as giving Bolivia access to the sea. The Chileans also sent a mission to Washington to persuade the US of the seriousness of the plan. This was enough to encourage the US to scrap the idea of referring the disputes immediately to the League. The Bolivians were not impressed. ' ... Chile was playing effectively to save time, since it knew of the unfavourable American public opinion towards joining the League,' wrote one diplomat and author later: 'Moreover, Wilson was totally absorbed with

> 'We still need another quarter of a century to make our preparations and then we will be invincible.'
> ISMAEL MONTES

solving European problems, since they were most relevant to the US interests at the time, while conflicts in the hemisphere, could, in Wilson's view, wait for a more appropriate time.'[3]

Peru and Bolivia now had little choice but to await the formal opening of the League when they could try to raise the issue again themselves. For Bolivia, raising the stakes on the dispute in any other way was unthinkable. There was no Bolivian keener to regain the country's lost lands than Ismael Montes, the man who had signed them away in a treaty. But for him there was an overriding foreign policy goal that – in the short term – was even more important than regaining a coastline. This was to avoid war, above all war with Chile. Setting out his arguments to La Paz, Montes said that there were parallels between their situation and recent events in Europe. *This country [Chile] is the most militarily prepared in South America. Its politics have been inspired along the same lines as those of Germany*, he wrote. Chile had enriched itself at the expense of its neighbours and it was prepared to fight new wars. Bolivia's aim was thus clear: *avoid war*. Otherwise, and even allowing for the bravery and heroism of its soldiers, Montes feared a *repetition of the disaster of '79* [the War of the Pacific]. In the meantime his country had to play for time, while they acquired the weapons and forces they needed with which to defend themselves. *We still need another quarter of a century to make our preparations and then we will be invincible* ... Nor did Montes give Bolivia much hope in a war with Chile even if Peru – which fought alongside it in the War of the Pacific – was again involved. *The old allies would be beaten as Peru, despite its appearance of military organisation, lacks efficiency in this respect.*[4]

Both countries therefore pressed ahead with attempts to raise their grievances at the League of Nations and soon ratified the Treaty of Versailles in their domestic legislature, the necessary prelude to becoming members of the new organisation. In Peru, for example, the text of the Treaty signed by Candamo in Paris on behalf of the government was put before the Peruvian national assembly on 25 September 1919 and approved on 17 November. Bolivia ratified the Treaty in the same month. This meant that both countries became founder members of the League when the Treaty came into force on 10 January 1920. Six days later the League, which had 42 founding members, held its first council meeting in Paris. Its first General Assembly meeting, however, did not take place until 15 November 1920, at the organisation's new permanent headquarters in Geneva.

Bolivia and Peru duly raised their respective disputes at the converted hotel that had become the League's new home. On 1 November, two weeks before the General Assembly met, the Bolivian delegation presented a request that the League consider their claim for access to the Pacific Ocean. On the same day Peru – represented in Geneva by García Calderón – also tabled its claim that the League's members should examine and revise the Treaty of Ancón that Peru had signed with Chile concerning Arica and Tacna. In its favour, Peru pointed to the new maxims of international law that condemned the taking of land by force, and also claimed that Chile's actions since the Ancón treaty – increasing the Chilean population, for example, to boost its chances of success if a local plebiscite on ownership were ever held – had effectively rendered it null and void. Both nations, however, were thwarted in their attempts. After much legalistic argument, the League's Secretary General Sir Eric Drummond – a British Foreign Office official who had been intimately involved with the organisation's creation in Paris – ruled that neither country had submitted their claims in time for them to be considered at the current meeting of the assembly. There is some suspicion that the League was worried that Chile might withdraw its membership if the cases were heard.

Neither country was impressed by the decision. Peru withdrew its request, though it reserved the right to make it again in the future, while Bolivia reluctantly agreed to postpone its request until the following year. It was not only the bureaucratic rules of the new organisation that frustrated the Bolivians. The Latin American solidarity that had been in such evidence during the Paris Peace Conference had clearly got lost in Geneva's autumnal fogs. Reporting back to La Paz, a member of the Bolivian team complained about the behaviour of the Central and South American delegates

THE LEAGUE OF NATIONS
The idea of a League of Nations did not originate with President Woodrow Wilson. However, he did become its most powerful proponent and he was determined to ensure that the Paris Peace Conference created such a body. In this he was successful, but stiff opposition back in America – where Republicans opposed many of the articles of the League, fearing they restricted American sovereignty – meant that the Treaty was never ratified and thus ensured that America never joined the very organisation it had pushed to establish. The absence of the powerful US helped doom the League to increasing irrelevance; it was to have some limited impact on relatively minor issues but was to prove helpless in areas such as the aggressive expansionist policies of Germany and Italy in the 1930s.

towards their claim, and in particular those from Brazil. The report bemoaned the fact that the 'the head of the Brazilian Mission was profoundly disagreeable to the Bolivian delegates'. Even more alarming was the whispered rumour from the Peruvian delegation that the Brazilian attitude 'conformed' with suggestions from the United States. The US, after all, was a country conspicuous by its absence at the Geneva meeting.[5]

The fact that the United States was not a member had come as little surprise to many observers, even though the organisation's most powerful backer in Paris had been President Wilson. As early as September 1919 Ecuador's Dorn had privately warned Quito from his Paris vantage point that domestic opposition to the American leader had *undermined the moral authority* of the entire Treaty of Versailles.[6] This opposition had been clear during the Peace Conference and had not diminished after the document was signed. Much of the opposition was to the terms of Article 10, under which members of the League undertook to 'respect and preserve' against external aggression the 'territorial integrity and existing political independence' of all members. For Wilson this article lay at the heart of the organisation's purpose. But for his opponents it undermined the role of the United States Congress and ultimately the American Constitution. An exhausting whistle-stop tour of the country by the ailing Wilson in September 1919 was unable to defeat this determined opposition and contributed to the President's worsening medical condition. Congress refused to ratify the Treaty and membership of the League and later in 1920 the Republican Warren Harding was voted into the White House, virtually guaranteeing that America would stay out of the League.

Even if the US's absence from the organisation was not

a shock, it was yet another blow to those Latin American nations who hoped the organisation would provide a check on their giant neighbour to the north. They had rested many of their hopes on Article 10 of the League's Covenant, the very article that had sparked US opposition. The refusal now of the US to join had two implications for Latin American countries. First, it gave Washington the freedom to act as it had always done in the region, without fear of provoking opposition among fellow League members. Secondly, there was the League's own reaction to the decision of the US to stay out. The League's first General Assembly in November had not exactly been greeted with a chorus of enthusiasm around the world. One British newspaper said that while in 1919 the start of the organisation's work had been eagerly awaited as an historic event of 'profound significance', the League was now little more than a 'sorry farce'. Reaction was little better in other key countries such as France and Italy. General Secretary Drummond was apparently worried that even his own country might follow the US and leave the League altogether. Thus the organisation had to play a delicate balancing act. It certainly had to reflect the views of its members, more than a quarter of whom were from Latin America. At the same time, it had no wish to antagonise the US, whose tacit support for much of the League's work could be very useful to it in the coming years. Ultimately, the League erred on the American side and was wary of becoming involved in issues the US felt were in its backyard.[7]

In these circumstances it is perhaps unsurprising that some Latin American members of the League developed rather a jaundiced view of the way it was run even in its infancy. In 1921 Argentina withdrew as a member after the Geneva-based body rejected its demand that its entire ruling

Council – whose permanent members had been decided at the Paris Peace Conference – should be voted by the Assembly members and that all sovereign nations should be allowed to be a member of the League. Buenos Aires did not resume full membership until 1933. In 1926, Brazil, which had been one of the non-permanent members of the Council, quit the League after its demand to be made a permanent council member was rejected. There was considerable irony here; it had, after all, been the Brazilian delegation at the Paris Peace Conference which had helped fight to boost the lesser powers' representation on both the League of Nations' Commission and its Council. In general, the behaviour of some Latin American delegates irritated other League members, not least because of their tendency to hold up Pan-American co-operation as a model for the way the League should behave.

Concerns at the League's ineffectiveness lay behind Peru's decision to seek a different solution to the Tacna-Arica issue. Lima now looked to US arbitration and ultimately bilateral talks with Chile to resolve the matter. This was far from straightforward, however, and it was not until 1929 that the parties finally reached an agreement. Tacna was handed back to Peruvian ownership, while Arica stayed with Chile.

Unfortunately for Bolivia it was not involved in this deal, and this meant the country was still left without access to the Pacific. Bolivia had tried to raise the matter a second time at the League of Nations shortly after its failure in 1920 and had also attempted to negotiate directly with Chile in 1923. Indeed, Santiago asked La Paz not to bring the issue up at the League a third time, in return for direct talks. Nothing came of either strategy. For the Bolivians the saga underlined its suspicion that the League was of little use; fear of alienating the US appeared to hamstring the organisation's actions. It also indicated that bilateral relations were also of limited use without Washington's backing. The Bolivians were convinced that that the US was at least partly responsible for its inability to reach a solution to the dispute. 'United States diplomacy accepted pragmatically that Chile and Peru deserved more attention than Bolivia, a country that was not only peripheral, but also was the weakest in the region,' noted one La Paz diplomat. In any case, neither Peru nor Bolivia could look upon their early experiences with the League of Nations with much fondness.[8]

Both countries were, however, still members of the League of Nations and the organisation again became involved in their affairs during the 1930s. In Peru's case it was over the small Amazonian town of Letica, an area that had been ceded to neighbouring Colombia back in 1922. In 1932, a group of heavily-armed Peruvians occupied the town and expelled Colombian officials. The League intervened in the conflict that followed, its Council opting to criticise Peru for its aggression. An agreement was eventually reached the following year under which the area was to be administered for a year by a League commission, albeit in the name of Colombia. The small, remote town had the distinction of seeing a specially devised League of Nations standard fluttering over it, the only time apart from the 1939 World's Fair when a flag was created for the organisation. The League intervened too in the bitter Chaco War between Bolivia and Paraguay in 1933 (see next chapter). At the urging of Britain's League of Nations minister Anthony Eden, who later became Foreign Secretary, the body organised an embargo among member states against selling arms to the warring countries. Eden later suggested that the League's actions had played a significant role in helping to stop the war.[9]

Of the four Spanish-speaking South American countries which signed the Treaty of Versailles, the biggest champion of the League was undoubtedly Uruguay. The country had already carved itself a niche as a venue for Pan-American meetings; it was not seen as a threat to other countries and was involved in few of the boundary disputes that punctuated South American diplomacy. Now, as the League began its work, Uruguay came to play a small but significant role in the organisation. In 1923, when the League Council's membership was enlarged to include more temporary members, Uruguay was elected to be Latin America's second representative alongside Brazil. The man chosen to sit on the Council on Uruguay's behalf was Juan Carlos Blanco, the country's minister in Paris and delegate at the Peace Conference.

'The election of our country onto the Executive Council is a great honour and it reflects the opinion that is held of us in Europe,' Blanco told a journalist in 1923.[10] His position gave him a ringside seat at an important episode in European history when French troops occupied the Ruhr region of Germany because of the latter's non-payment of war reparations. 'The Council is watching events closely,' was all that a guarded Blanco would tell the Uruguayan press at the time. In fact there was little else he could say, as the League was powerless to act.

'A united America is not merely an ideal ... but an economic and social reality.'
JUAN BUERO

Uruguay's other delegate at Paris, Juan Antonio Buero, also became involved in the League's work. After finishing his term as Foreign Minister in 1923 the experienced international lawyer later went on to become his country's legal advisor at the League as well as having a spell in his country's Senate. Buero had already shown his appreciation of the organisation's work back in July 1922 when he and President Brum called for the creation of a League of Nations for the Americas. Speaking in advance of the Fifth International Conference of American States, Buero said their idea for a *League of American Nations* should be based on the *absolute equality of all of them*; its advantages including enabling the continent to co-ordinate its views ahead of other world meetings. He said, *… if as we wish the League is formed … the Americas will become ever stronger and more closely united in the League. We could discuss our American affairs and prepare ourselves to act in harmony at great conferences where affairs of the whole world are under discussion.* The loquacious Buero then waxed lyrical about the continent and its importance to the world. *America is the rejuvenating force of Western civilisation. It has always borne the proud title of the land of freedom. It may also justly be styled the land of hope.* American countries did not just export raw materials to Europe, but also the continent's *healthy optimism, the community of interests, ideals and hopes … a united America is not merely an ideal … but an economic and social reality.* Buero cited the concrete example of greater economic ties between the US and Latin America. *Business between North and South America, which formerly was only a question of comparatively small sums, has increased enormously since the war.*[11]

Buero and Brum's plan for a League of American Nations was duly raised at the Santiago Conference in 1923. The idea generated sufficient interest for it to be sent to the Governing Board of the Pan-American Union for more detailed consideration, but nothing came of it. Despite Buero's fine words about growing American unity, there was little real sign at the Santiago Conference that US relations with the

Latin American states had matured and grown more harmonious. The view that the Latin American countries had of Washington and international bodies was now coloured by their experiences of the war, their participation in the Paris Peace Conference, and their membership of the League of Nations. The only real achievement of the Santiago gathering was to agree a mechanism to resolve disputes between member countries. Uruguay's dream of a 'united America' was to remain just that.

When Enrique Dorn y de Alsua signed the Treaty of Versailles on 28 June 1919 on his country's behalf, it seemed as if Ecuador, too, like Peru, Bolivia and Uruguay, was destined to take up a seat as a founder member of the League, However, the country's hopes of membership were almost dashed even before the Treaty was signed. The bondholders in the Guayaquil and Quito Railway had not given up hope of using the Paris Peace Conference as a platform to complain about Ecuador's refusal to pay its debts. Another angry letter from the well-connected bondholders to Lord Curzon at the Foreign Office back in London had some impact. In May 1919 the aristocrat wrote to Arthur Balfour in Paris, pointing out that the bondholders wanted the issue taken up directly with the Ecuadorian delegate – Dorn.

Curzon wondered whether any countries that 'wilfully defaulted' on their foreign obligations should be barred from joining the League of Nations. 'It is understood that Mexico will not be admitted and though her case is worse than that of Ecuador, her exclusion might form a precedent to some extent for similar treatment in the case of the latter,' he wrote. There was also talk of the matter being raised with Sir Eric Drummond, who would be the League's first Secretary General. Balfour, however, was clear that Ecuador could not be excluded at this late stage. 'I fear the moment has passed,' he wrote to Lord Curzon. The Covenant on the formation of the League agreed by the Peace Conference on 28 April had constituted a 'formal invitation' to Ecuador, as it did to other participants to join the League, '… this is an invitation which it seems impossible now to withdraw.' Instead Balfour suggested that Ecuador be pressured to accept arbitration under the Hague Convention, and that if it refused 'Ecuador would be compelled by her obligations under the covenant to submit her dispute with His Majesty's Government to an arbitral tribunal or to the Council of the League.[12]

In fact, what neither Lord Curzon nor Balfour could have known at this time was that Ecuador would not become a member of the League of Nations when it started work in 1920 and would not become so until 1934. The reason for this was that Ecuador, despite taking part in the Paris Peace Conference, and despite Dorn's signature on 28 June, did not ratify the Treaty of Versailles. The end of the war had brought difficult times in Ecuador, partly because the price of cacao had suddenly collapsed. That, combined with political turbulence meant that foreign affairs – especially if not directly involving border issues – were hardly a priority. Over the ensuing decade or so Ecuador would rein back on most of its overseas representation. Ironically, it was only after seeing Colombia and Peru reach an agreement over land Ecuador claimed that Quito chose to appeal to the League for help. The League could not help, as Ecuador was not a member. The country finally ratified the Treaty on 18 September 1934, allowing it to join. In hindsight Dorn's presence at the Paris Peace Conference seemed to have been largely in vain, and his excitement about what it would mean for his country sadly premature.

7

Revolution and Nationalism

For countries such as France and Belgium, it was all too apparent how the First World War had marked their countries forever. Wounded former soldiers and the destruction wrought on buildings and landscapes were grisly testament to that. Europe was not alone, though, in being changed by the conflict. South America may have had no old trenches, no visible scars in the mud nor walking wounded. Yet the conflict did bring about changes in Ecuador, Uruguay, Bolivia and Peru, as it did throughout the rest of South America. On a wider level pre-war British domination in trade and finance was being challenged. American influence, which had already been on the increase, would grow stronger. But the volatility of South American economies caused by the disruption of the war also had important effects on the ground, among ordinary people.

One of the most significant effects was growing unrest among the urban and working classes across Latin America, including Ecuador, Peru and Bolivia. Fluctuations in trade and government efforts to remedy them led to rising inflation. This affected the price of basic foodstuffs as well as other goods and led to a fall in the real earning power of wages; a potentially combustible combination. If these were the practical causes of unrest, there was an ideological side too. The Russian Revolution of 1917 had cast a deep shadow over the Paris Peace Conference and its influence was also felt in Latin America. Though there was little likelihood of a communist-inspired revolution occurring, the events in Russia served as an inspiration for the region's working classes. The suffering caused by economic disruption in the war coupled with the harmful trade restrictions of countries such as Britain also hammered home the risks of over-reliance on overseas finance and foreign companies. The end of the war thus marked the end of a golden period of economic liberalism, notably in the Andean Republics. A new era was beginning, marked more by nationalism and a state-driven approach to economics and society.

For a brief period after the war it looked, however, as if Ecuador might resist the political and economic changes that were sweeping the region. José Luis Tamayo, a lawyer from the Radical Liberal party, elected in 1920, was very much a business-as-usual president, promising little or no break with the policies of the past. Having worked as a lawyer for the local banks, he knew them well and understood the grip they and coastal plantation owners had on trade and commerce. Together this network of banks and plantation owners was known as the *argolla* or 'ring'. The president's concept of reform was simply to tell the banks, 'Gentlemen, content yourself with less profit.' In interviews with the foreign press, Tamayo admitted that his country's finances were in the 'worst possible condition' but said he wanted to put these on a stable footing; he committed himself to 'encouraging the investment of foreign capital in the country', though he also conceded that he had an 'uphill task ahead'.[1]

Tamayo was right about the last part. A triple combination of a falling share in the world cacao market in the face of competition from African competitors, lower prices and then in 1922 a severe outbreak of blight heralded the end of Ecuador's age of chocolate. Fortunes were lost, landowners sold their land or left it abandoned and plantation workers joined forces with their urban counterparts in a series of strikes and unrest over low wages, jobs losses and inflation. Faced with these disturbances, the authorities reacted brutally. When a general strike led by local bakers and other workers was called in Guayaquil on 15 November 1922, a large number of protestors were gunned down. At least 300 people were killed, many of them thrown into the river after having their bodies cut open to stop them floating. Some reports put the figure as high as 1,000 or more killed. The following year a group of small peasant farmers or *campesinos* were massacred around the town of Ambato.

The fear of even more widespread unrest led the country's ruling Liberals to change their style of governing. They drew up plans for state intervention to regulate prices, for syndicates to represent (and thus control) workers and professionals, and for better medical care and housing. However, they were unable to agree on the right candidate to carry through these modest reforms. The party mainstream chose Gonzalo Córdoba as its man for the 1924 presidential elections, another politician who had strong links with the influential bank owners. More radical Liberals backed Colonel Juan Manuel Lasso, who was soon winning popular support among the working classes as well as disgruntled members of the increasingly influential middle classes. Crucially, he had the support of many lower-ranking army officers, many of whom were drawn from the ranks of the working and middle classes. Lasso should have won the election comfortably, as even some Conservatives switched support from their own candidate to back him. But the outgoing government labelled Lasso an extremist, and in a rigged election Córdova was declared as the winner. The grim joke was that Lasso lost the election because he was too popular. It was the death-knell of the years of Liberal rule. An ailing Córdova was poorly equipped to handle the growing unrest, and it was no huge surprise when on 9 July 1925 a group of young army officers seized power in a bloodless coup, an event known after the month as the *juliano*.

The League of Young Military Officers aimed to root out corruption and end the dominance of the coastal banks over the economy; four were closed, their assets were seized and a number of bankers were banished abroad. The coup also marked a shift in power back to the sierra and Quito and away from Guayaquil and the coast. The military soon handed power over to a civilian, Isidro Ayora, an obstetrician from Quito who had married into a wealthy family from the coast. Over the next few years he set about dismantling the *argolla* and introduced reforms to help, among other groups, teachers and public sector workers.

As part of his reforms, Ayora brought in a team of financial experts led by the American academic Edwin W. Kemmerer. The Princeton professor was known for his consistent – some said inflexible – approach to such reforms, and his blueprint for Ecuador included the establishment of a central bank in the capital Quito. This and other reforms were identical to those Kemmerer and his team had already proposed for other countries. Indeed, so formatted was the approach that one of the officials simply copied, word for word, the customs code he had written for Paraguay (whose international trade was carried via river) and applied it to Ecuador (whose water-ways were domestic). Despite this unpromising start, much of Kemmerer's approach was adopted, including the creation of a central bank. Ayora and his ministers hoped that the American academic's presence would encourage foreign investment, something the country still needed, even if it was wary about the dangers of reliance on outside forces. The US, however, coloured by the Guayaquil and Quito Railway experience, continued to see Ecuador as a poor value, high-risk investment. During the 1920s just 0.3 per cent of direct US investment in Latin America found its way into Ecuador. This was not helped by the fact that it took a sceptical Washington three years to recognise the new regime in Ecuador. Not even the help of a distinguished Princeton academic could change American investment habits.

The advent of the Depression in the 1930s made Ecuador's already difficult situation even worse. The ailing cacao trade slumped yet further and there was little sign that the country was capable of developing an industrial base, as was happening in some other parts of the continent. One of the reasons was a lack of infrastructure. By the end of the 1930s the country had just 4,000 cars, thanks to a wretched road network, and just over 600 miles of railway. Inflation rose and government revenues fell. The political situation mirrored the country's economic plight. Ayora's inability to tackle the country's problems saw him removed by the army in 1931 and there followed a period of extraordinary political instability. The stark facts tell the story; from 1925 to 1947 Ecuador had 23 different presidents, none of whom finished his scheduled term in office. In one three-month period in 1933, the government managed to get through no fewer than 12 foreign ministers. The key political figure to emerge out of the chaos was

José Maria Velasco Ibarra who in 1934 began the first of what would turn out to be no fewer than five terms as president. An opportunist with a gift for communication, Ibarra stayed at the centre of Ecuadorian politics for decades; his last term of office ended in 1972. However, even this accomplished vote-winner could do little to solve the country's crippling economic problems or its political and social unrest. Nor could he prevent Ecuador's catastrophic boundary war.

It was Ibarra who reversed the foreign policy of Ecuador and took the country into the League of Nations in 1934, a decade and a half after it had spurned the chance to become a founder member. Its conversion to international organisations was so complete that Quito even picked up on Uruguay's old idea and called for a Latin America League of Nations, though to little avail. Instead it soon found itself at conflict with Peru.

Ever since independence the two countries had argued over their borders, which were poorly defined in the Amazon region. In particular Ecuador claimed a stretch of land north of the River Marañón, which would give it access to the River Amazon and an outlet to the Atlantic. Ecuador had already suffered the loss of land to Peru, Colombia and Brazil in the past and was in no mood to compromise on its claims. However, Peru had also lost territory, to Chile and Colombia, and refused to cede an inch more land. Militarily, the countries were a mismatch. Both countries had employed Italian military advisers but the Peruvian armed forces were far bigger and better equipped. Nonetheless in the late 1930s Ecuador remained defiant and even sent troops to the border of an area that Peru had governed since independence. The public mood in Ecuador demanded there be no compromise. War eventually broke out in July 1941 after a group of

Peruvian farmers accidentally strayed into Ecuadorian territory and were fired on by troops.

The war lasted just three weeks and the Ecuadorians were beaten by the larger and better-trained and equipped Peruvian force, who then occupied a southern province of Ecuador. Quito appealed to the US for help but Washington soon had other matters on its mind; the Japanese attacked Pearl Harbor in December. Ecuadorian demonstrated its solidarity with the US when in early January 1942 it became one of the first Latin American nations to break off relations with Germany and Japan. But the US had no intention of getting distracted by the Ecuadorian dispute. With the help of Brazilian diplomacy, Peru and a reluctant Ecuador signed the Rio de Janeiro Protocol of January 1942. Under this Ecuador gave up its claims to more than 80,000 square miles of unoccupied land in the Amazon, plus 5,000 square miles of occupied land.

The defeat was a huge blow to national pride. It was also a major blow to the president Carlos Alberto Arroyo del Río, who had ruled Ecuador since 1939. Both he and the US were blamed for Ecuador's humiliation, and though the President clung to power for a while despite violent protests, his days in office were numbered. On 28 May 1944 there was an uprising among sections of the military. Faced with a broad coalition of opponents, from communists to conservatives, Arroyo del Río fled to the US. In Ecuador this revolution is known as *la gloriosa*. It was seen as a 'glorious effort by the Ecuadorian people to reclaim their national dignity, their pride in being Ecuadorian'.[2] Meanwhile, Ecuador generally adopted a pro-Allied line during the war, though it did not declare war on the Axis Powers. Both the South American country and the United States feared a declaration of war could provoke an attack by the enemy on Ecuador. In particular the United

States wanted to ensure that the Galápagos Islands remained in friendly hands, and with Ecuador's agreement, Washington established a military base on one of the islands during the war. For America this provided protection for the crucial Panama Canal. For Ecuador it provided protection against potential attack from Japan – or its neighbour Peru. The base was dismantled after the war ended and for a decade, thanks to increasing banana exports, Ecuador experienced a period of boom and bust economically and relative stability politically, at least compared with the immediate pre-war years.

At his comfortable Parisian home, Enriquez Dorn y de Alsua was less affected than most Ecuadorians by the economic and political troubles of his country after the First World War. He had continued with his diplomatic duties, for example representing his country on an International Convention on the naming of illnesses and diseases held in Paris in October 1920. Through his friendship with Pierre de Coubertin, Dorn also served as Ecuador's first International Olympic Committee member until 1929. The wealthy diplomat's life was not without tribulations even in his twilight days, though. In 1934 the Stavisky affair broke in Paris, a scandal involving fraud, politicians and the upper echelons of society, and one that rocked France's Third Republic. At the centre of the affair was a Russian, Alexandre Stavisky, who had apparently fraudulently amassed a fortune in France. Stavisky died in 1934 – it was either suicide or murder according to different accounts – after which the scandal broke in public. During his time in Paris Stavisky had used a number of prominent and well-connected people as screens for his activities. One unwitting victim was the well-off and well-connected Dorn. Unable to race horses under his own name because of his chequered past, Stavisky raced them in the colours of the Ecuadorian.

Though there is no evidence that Dorn was involved in any wrongdoing himself, his connection with the affair was publicised and his reputation affected. However, the impact on his good name could have been worse were it not for some behind-the-scenes lobbying on his behalf. Jean Contoux Montalvo, son of a renowned Ecuadorian writer whom Dorn had known in the 1880s when living in Paris, and who remembered the old diplomat with fondness from his childhood when he used to bounce him on his knee, pleaded the old man's case with some success among friends who worked for the Parisian press. To his dying day, however, Dorn never found out about the service the young man had done him.[3]

> 'The people of Uruguay have always known how to reciprocate the consideration of those nations who have ever evinced towards them a high respect and a friendly attitude.'
>
> JUAN BUERO

Having taken up the post of foreign minister in March 1919, Juan Buero was far more closely involved in his country's day-to-day affairs than was Dorn. Thanks to his presence at the Paris Peace Conference, Buero was on friendly terms with such powerful men as President Woodrow Wilson. In February 1920 he and his wife Alda went on an official trip to Washington, where the couple were greeted by Wilson's wife Edith, the President himself still recovering from a stroke he had suffered late the previous year. Before that, in November 1919, Buero had been to London to head a Uruguayan delegation. This was a return visit for the 1918 British mission to South America led by Sir Maurice de Bunsen. In a typically flamboyant speech, Buero spoke of Uruguay's *genuine admiration* for Britain's *liberal institutions* and said that the country realised that it owed much of its material progress to British co-operation. *The people of Uruguay have always known how to reciprocate the consideration of those nations who have ever evinced towards them a high respect and a friendly attitude*, he told his audience.[4]

After his term as foreign minister ended, Buero remained a prominent figure in Uruguayan public life. In the mid-1920s he was briefly president of the Senate and it was in this capacity that in April 1925 he welcomed a famous visitor to the country – Albert Einstein. In a speech of welcome to the Senate, Buero compared Einstein to other great scientists of the past, such as Kepler, Galileo and Newton. *His human presence is so tangible that it is, in its way almost incredible, when you think of the enormous significance of his concepts of mechanics and philosophy in their application to all human knowledge.* The Senate president also made clear to their illustrious guest how proud they were to receive him, and suggested that the visit gave Uruguay a chance to show that, despite its size, it did not lack ambition. The Senate's welcome was a *demonstration that in this part of America, and despite the modesty of our scientific community, we also follow with admiration and affection his successful attempt to reveal the great mystery of the world.*[5]

Buero's career continued to flourish, even if he would never again hold high office in government. After a spell as his country's legal advisor to the League of Nations and as a senator, in 1935 he joined the Permanent Court of Arbitration in The Hague. He lived to witness the next world war and died in 1950, when he was still only 62. Though a great orator and gifted lawyer and diplomat, he left behind very few writings.

Buero was not the only one in his family to make a mark in public life. His brother Enrique E. Buero was also an international lawyer and diplomat, and after the Second World War became Uruguayan Ambassador in London. But perhaps his most important contribution – in a country that loves the sport – was his role in creating the first football World Cup. In 1925 Enrique Buero was Uruguay's minister in Brussels and during a visit to Geneva he met Jules Rimet, the President of the world football organisation FIFA. The two men agreed that to celebrate the game's success, there should be some form of world tournament and Buero later became vice-president of FIFA. In 1929 a FIFA congress met in Barcelona to choose the venue for the proposed World Cup. With the support of other Latin American countries, Uruguay, whose delegate was Dr Héctor Rivadavia Gómez, won the vote. It was also agreed that the tournament would coincide with the centenary of the country's first constitution. The tournament was not without its problems, and only four teams from Europe took part. A number of European countries grumbled it was too far to travel and were also worried about what they feared would be the harsh conditions of a Southern Hemisphere winter. Notable absentees were Spain and Italy, despite the fact that most Uruguayans were descended from one or other of those two countries. Yet the tournament of 13 nations went ahead, and to the hosts' immense joy they won the event, beating Argentina 4–2 in the final before a crowd of 93,000. As a satisfied Jules Rimet left after the final he declared: 'I sincerely congratulate those who had the initiative of organizing the championship here; Messrs Gomez and Buero, as their negotiation ability was the exclusive factor in obtaining the vote of the Congress of Barcelona …'.[6]

A year before the inaugural World Cup, the country's dominant politician of his generation, José Batlle y *Ordóñez*, had died. Batlle had overseen a remarkable transformation in his Uruguay, from a country split by bitter and often bloody political rivalry to the region's first welfare state. In the provision of education – including for women – pensions, paid holidays and minimum wages, Uruguay led the way on the continent both during Batlle's lifetime and afterwards. However, Batlle knew that for his reforms to work they had to be accepted both by the political classes and the people. He had long believed that one of the causes of the country's past divisions had been unfair elections and dictatorially-minded presidents. His most controversial proposal, therefore, was a major reform of the country's system of government.

Batlle had briefly been interim president at the end of the 19th century and then served two terms from 1903–7 and from 1911–15. In between these two spells, and in common with many Latin American leaders who left office, the Uruguayan had spent time in Europe. Here he had been struck by the form of government in Switzerland, which instead of having a powerful executive president was ruled under a collegiate system. Batlle became determined to introduce this approach into Uruguay, an ambitious project even for one with his authority. His plans for an Executive Council to replace the country's president were indeed rejected at first. Not just the opposition Blancos but sections of his own Colorado Party were unhappy about the proposal. In 1917 the charismatic leader had eventually secured a compromise deal under which a new constitution came into force in 1919. Uruguay would still have a president, who would handle foreign affairs, defence and internal security. But most domestic issues such as the economy, health, education and industry were to be overseen by a National Council of Administration, consisting of nine elected members. A third of these faced election every two years, with each individual serving no more than six years in total. The voting system was devised in such a way to ensure that the opposition Blancos – officially known as the National Party – always had some representation on the Council. This was an attempt to make them feel included in the system. The first president to hold power under this so-called *colegiado* system was Baltasar Brum, the man who appointed Buero as foreign minister.

The new constitution did not stop there. It also separated Church and state, gave greater autonomy for local authorities and provided for a secret ballot at elections. Despite the compromise, the new system was not to everyone's liking. The *colegiado* was to become a fault line in Uruguayan politics and remained a controversial issue for decades to come. The system worked well enough in the 1920s as Uruguay enjoyed a period of relative prosperity and calm. But the Depression hit the country's exports, and Uruguay's economy began to suffer amid growing unrest.

By 1933 the Colorado Party president Gabriel Terra had come to the conclusion that the National Council was not part of the solution to his country's problems but part of the problem. It was slow, cumbersome and, in his view, carrying out policies that were simply not going to tackle the growing crisis. On 31 March Terra, with the backing of Luis Alberto de Herrera from the rival Blanco party, staged a bloodless coup d'état, dissolving both the National Council and the legislature, and ruling by decree. It was a dramatic move, even more so because Uruguay appeared to have put its years of turbulent governance behind it. The coup also profoundly shocked many of those who had stayed loyal to Batlle's policies. Baltasar Brum was so appalled that he committed suicide. Yet Terra succeeded in winning support for a new constitution, which switched most of the National Council's powers back to the president and instead established a Cabinet that contained both Colorado and Blanco politicians. This was not the end of the constitutional wrangles, however. In 1942 Uruguay adopted a fresh constitution, followed by yet another a decade later. This installed a system close to Batlle's original *colegiado* proposal, and under which the head of the government was the President of the National Council. This reform was not to prove a lasting success, either, but many years after his death, Batlle's legacy was continuing to have a major impact on Uruguayan political affairs.

In foreign affairs Uruguay continued its support for international organisations, including the League of Nations and the regular International Conferences of American States. The seventh of these was held in Montevideo in December 1933, and provided a chance for the host's diplomats to play their part in improving US–Latin American relations. Earlier that year the new US president Franklin Roosevelt had articulated what became known as America's 'Good Neighbor' foreign policy and the Montevideo conference provided a chance for the Washington administration to show it meant business. The outcome was considered a success, thanks in some small part to Uruguayan diplomacy.

THE GOOD NEIGHBOR POLICY
Latin American nations had long been suspicious of the US's motives, those suspicions seemingly justified by its interventions in the region. This concern grew after Washington helped Cuba achieve independence from Spain in the Spanish-American War of 1898. From the late 1920s the US gradually began to adjust its policy, culminating in the so-called Good Neighbor Policy espoused by President Franklin Roosevelt in 1933. This put the focus on co-operation and mutual trust rather than on unilateral intervention in Latin American countries. The Good Neighbor Policy helped to improve US-Latin American relations as world conflict loomed in the late 1930s.

One academic observer wrote: 'It is generally agreed that the Montevideo conference went further towards creating genuine goodwill than any preceding Pan-American conference ... it represented a turning point in the history of the movement.'[7]

Uruguay's response to the Second World War bore strong similarities to its attitude in the First World War. The sympathy of the government and much of the populace was with the Allies. As in the earlier conflict, there were rumours of a German plot to overthrow the government. In December 1939 Uruguay became involved in one of the most famous naval episodes of the early part of the war. The German 'pocket battleship' *Admiral Graf Spee* – named after the German admiral who had gone down with his ship off the Falkland Islands in the First World War – had been attacking Allied shipping in the Atlantic Ocean. The cruiser was finally tracked down and confronted by three Royal Navy cruisers off the coast of Uruguay on 13 December 1939, and during what became known as the Battle of the River Plate the *Graf Spee* was damaged. The German vessel went into Montevideo's port for repairs. But this was a neutral port, and under international law the *Graf Spee* was not allowed to spend more than 24 hours in harbour. Following British representations, the Uruguayan authorities informed the German ship's captain that if it was not gone within 72 hours the vessel would be interned. Faced with what seemed like overwhelming odds against the Royal Navy, her captain sailed the *Graf Spee* out into the Río Plata estuary and scuttled her.

Uruguay broke off relations with the Axis Powers in January 1942, a month after Pearl Harbor, and put its ports at the disposal of Allied navies. It formally declared war on the Axis Powers in February 1945. Not everyone, however, approved of Uruguay's pro-Allied stance. The opposition leader Luis Alberto Herrera felt the country should be more concerned about US dominance of the region than the remote threat from Germany, and favoured a policy of neutrality. His views chimed with many in Argentina, where some politicians and military officers went even further, appearing to favour an Axis victory. Though Uruguay was usually at great pains to remain on good terms with its powerful neighbours, this differing approach to the war contributed to a growing tension between Montevideo and Buenos Aires. This continued after the war during the regime of Argentine President Juan Perón, when Uruguay offered political asylum to political refugees from across the Río Plata.

The political scene in Bolivia at the end of the First World War was very different from that of Uruguay. Ismael Montes's successor as president, José Gutiérrez Guerra, essentially carried on the same policies that the country had followed for two decades. But support from the business community was ebbing away from the Liberals while the new Republican Party was growing in power. When in 1920 Gutiérrez tried to designate his successor in the presidential elections the Republicans staged a coup – one without bloodshed – and ended Liberal rule. This coup was a remarkably civilised affair. Gutiérrez, who had been educated in Britain, cheerfully told *The Times'* man in La Paz that he had no objection to being deported – though he preferred to be sent to Chile rather than Peru. In any case he said his aim was to return to live in England, though in fact he took up a banking job in America. Later he said he would not return to a land where 'only exotic plants abound and few noble souls are to be found'. Meanwhile the new man in charge, Bautista Saavedra, reassured *The Times'* correspondent that that the deposed politician would be safe, adding, 'Bolivians don't eat Bolivians'. The arrival of the Republicans in power did not however mark a radical change in politics in Bolivia, simply a change of personnel at the top. As one observer put it: 'Twenty years of privilege for one group ends and ten years of privilege for another begins.'[8]

An early warning sign of the gradual disintegration of Bolivian politics came when the Republicans split into different factions soon after seizing power. The man who had emerged as the dominant figure was Saavedra, an intellectual with an autocratic style. He recognised that there were sectors in the country who were demanding to be heard, the lower middle classes and the working classes. Saavedra set up government conciliation schemes to solve industrial disputes and began a programme of public works to modernise the country's cities. But there was little action to ease the plight of the largely ignored Indian communities. Efforts to win support among workers also suffered a terrible setback when government troops were involved in a massacre of miners at Uncía in 1923. Nor did Saavedra endear himself to the powerful mining lobby when he raised extra taxes on tin exports, prompting a disgusted Simon Patiño to move the headquarters of his tin empire to the US. Saavedra's efforts to raise foreign loans to finance infrastructure programmes – which effectively handed control over Bolivian taxes to US interests – also caused widespread national anger.

Saavedra's successor as president, Hernando Siles, who created his own National Party in the mid-1920s, presided over greater fragmentation of Bolivian politics and a worsening economic climate. Gradually the voices of students, Indian groups and new parties of the left were beginning to be heard, even though their numbers were still small and their direct influence very limited. An important figure supporting the Indian cause was Tristan Marof (real name Gustavo Navarro), a diplomat who saw in Bolivia's Inca heritage a blueprint for a modern state. In a 1926 book he promoted Inca socialism and rejected the 'individualistic, capitalist bourgeois way of life' that had been imported from outside. Communism was not a new philosophy, he said, 'centuries ago the Incas practised it with the greatest success ... '. It was a philosophy that would find powerful advocates in the Andean Republics in the years ahead.[9] When in 1930 Siles tried to extend his time in office he was deposed by sections of the military, and Saavedra's bitter rival Daniel Salamanca eventually came to power. On top of the country's existing problems, Salamanca also had to deal with the effects of the Depression. As an exporting country Bolivia was quickly hit by the economic slump, and tin exports and revenues fell. It was a hard situation for any politician to tackle, even someone as confident as Salamanca who had long believed he was the man destined to lead his country to greatness. As the economic situation worsened and political opposition to his domestic policies grew, Salamanca turned much of his attention to foreign issues, and especially his country's border with Paraguay. But the result of this focus on Bolivia's south-eastern frontier was to have catastrophic consequences for the country.

The 1929 agreement between Peru and Chile over Tacna and Arica seemed to preclude – for the moment – any chance that land-locked Bolivia would regain its Pacific outlet. Attention turned instead eastwards towards the Atlantic Ocean. Oil companies were now searching for deposits in parts of Bolivia and politicians and businessmen flirted with the idea of a pipeline to the River Paraguay from where – it was thought – tankers could ship the oil to the sea. There was just one problem. The area between Bolivia and the river – known as the Chaco – belonged to Paraguay. Despite Bolivia's precarious finances, Salamanca began a military build-up along the border of the Chaco region and tension with Paraguay rose. In 1931 Bolivia broke off diplomatic relations with its neighbour and in July 1932 Salamanca claimed that Paraguayan forces had seized a Bolivian military installation. The Chaco War had begun.

It is widely believed that Salamanca deliberately provoked the Paraguayans into war. Many see it as a classic attempt to divert attention from the country's domestic problems and unite the country behind him in a foreign adventure where Salamanca could at last claim the glory he believed was his right. If so, then it backfired spectacularly and tragically. Paraguay, which in a particularly bloody 19th-century war had lost land to both Brazil and Argentina, was determined not to relinquish its hold on the Chaco. As for Bolivia, its military suffered from long supply chains, the country's Andean soldiers were unused to fighting on the low-altitude terrain of the Chaco and its military commanders seemed to have little confidence in their president. The Paraguayans not only repulsed the Bolivian offensive but counter-attacked themselves, and in the second half of 1934 even threatened Bolivia's own oil fields. In November 1934 a furious Salamanca went to the military headquarters to try to effect a change of leadership. In the event it was the military who did that, arresting the President and forcing him to stand down.

By now both countries were militarily exhausted, and Paraguay in particular had financial problems. In June 1935 the two sides signed a peace treaty, and final agreement on a settlement was reached in 1938. Bolivia was forced to give up

50,000 square miles of territory and renounce claims to the lands bordering the Paraguay River. The human toll in what was the biggest conflict in the Americas since the American Civil War was immense. Bolivia lost up to 60,000 men, while Paraguay suffered around 37,000 casualties. Politically and socially, the war also had far-reaching consequences within Bolivia. The final remains of the political system that had existed under the Liberals and had begun to fade under the Republicans were now swept away as the Bolivian public was filled with a deep sense of mistrust in the old Bolivian ruling classes. Parties on the left became more vocal, and there was a widespread appetite for change. It was also widely believed – though there is no evidence for this – that the Chaco War was provoked at the behest of the US oil firm Standard Oil. This chimed with the views of men such as Tristan Marof that the problem facing countries such as Bolivia and its Indian peoples was exploitation by outsiders. The waste and terrible handling of the war even inspired a whole genre of Chaco novels.

After the Chaco War debacle Bolivia was led by a succession of military rulers. Colonel David Toro was in power long enough to nationalise Standard Oil – a popular move – in 1937 before another officer, Germán Busch, staged a coup and seized power. Busch had been one of the few military leaders to emerge from the Chaco War with credit and was determined to move more quickly with the corporatist reforms of his predecessor. He saw through new labour legislation, and in 1939 he issued a decree that all foreign exchange earnings from tin exports had to go to the government. It would then distribute the monies back to the mines for vital investments. However, Busch committed suicide later that year and was eventually replaced in 1940 by another war veteran, General

Enrique Penaranda. He was the candidate backed by Liberal and Republican factions, and his election win hinted at a possible return to the old days. But Bolivia had changed. The defeated candidate in the 1940 poll was a Marxist university lecturer José Antonio Arze. Despite the fact that he was virtually unknown and had just a few weeks to campaign, Arze received nearly 10,000 of the 60,000 available votes under the country's limited voting franchise. Then 1941 saw the creation of the National Revolutionary Party (MNR in Spanish), the country's first mass appeal party, which brought together academics, workers and the middle classes. The MNR stood against both capitalism and Marxism, was nationalistic and opposed what it saw as foreign economic imperialism.

General Penaranda and the US government labelled the MNR as Nazi sympathisers and its party leaders were gaoled, exiled or forced into hiding in the second half of 1941. But the limited popularity of the government – which was pro-Allies and which broke off relations with Germany and Japan in January 1942 – was already waning, not least because of another terrible massacre of mine workers, one of the worst in the country's history, that took place at the Catavi tin mine in December 1942. The following year MNR leaders reached a deal with disgruntled junior officers in the military, who seized power. The new president was yet another veteran of the Chaco War, Major Gaulberto Villarroel. But this time his government included members of the MNR in the cabinet, including its influential figure Víctor Paz Estenssoro at the treasury. This was the first government in recent decades not to include members of the traditional 'elite', and it pursued policies intended to help urban workers and Indians. It was also a government sympathetic to the Axis powers. However, the dictatorial Villarroel alienated many sections of society, and by the end of the Second World War his authoritarian style looked very out of date. In 1946 he was removed from office and publicly lynched on the streets. Six years later, however, the MNR – by then shorn of any pro-fascist leanings it may have had – would be back in power as it began one of Latin America's most far-reaching social revolutions.

Ismael Montes did not live to see Bolivia's 1952 revolution. However, the end of the Paris Peace Conference had not meant the end of public life for the former president, whatever he may have suggested at the time. Indeed he was unwittingly thrust into the limelight in 1920 when the Republicans took power and very publicly disowned Montes as their representative in France. According to a Bolivian statement to the US State Department the ex-president had 'unrightfully' kept hold of the archives from the legation in France and was using the title of 'Minister to France' even though the new regime said he had 'ceased to merit the confidence' of the Bolivian government. This diplomatic banishment owed much to the fracture of Liberal Party over the previous years and Montes' strained relations with Republican Party leaders. He therefore spent the next eight years in exile. Montes later returned to Bolivia but fell out with President Siles, accusing the latter of trying to keep in power at any cost. The president tried to have the veteran politician arrested, but Montes managed to gain the protection of Chilean diplomats and left the country.

'This is my revenge.'
ISMAEL MONTES

From abroad he helped topple Siles's regime, and returned to La Paz in 1930.[10]

For a brief period it looked as if Montes would once more play a prominent role in Bolivian politics. He was chosen as a vice-president but soon stood down, apparently under pressure from powerful elements in the military. He was however still chairman of the Central Bank, which helped to finance the Chaco War, and was an enthusiastic supporter of the war effort. In October 1932 he visited troops at the front and declared that morale was *excellent*. Montes also revealed a bleak sense of humour. The former president had publicly backed Salamanca for the presidency in 1931, even though the two men had been political enemies for a long time and were not on speaking terms. At the time the economy was in a dire condition, and when asked, given their enmity, why he had supported Salamanca, Montes is said to have responded: *This is my revenge.* If so, he did not have much time to enjoy it. Montes died in November 1933 following another trip to the Chaco front. His right leg had become gangrenous, and though doctors amputated it, it was too late to save the ageing statesman.

The immediate post-First World War period saw Peru facing serious economic and social problems. Even as Candamo and García Calderón prepared for the Peace Conference in January 1919, back home in Lima and Callao there was a three-day general strike, supported by the increasingly influential students at San Marcos University. It was part of a pattern seen across much of Latin America at this time; inflation and a reduction in real spending power leading to protests and strikes. Yet despite the evidence of the January strikes, Peru was not on the eve of a period of political instability. In 1919 the former president Augusto Leguía returned from five years in London and won the election to replace President José Pardo. Not content with winning the poll, Leguía and his followers staged a coup on 4 July, alleging that Pardo and others were plotting to stop him taking up office. The real reason was probably that it gave Leguía the chance to arrange a congress that was more favourable to him. In any case the diminutive but energetic president was to stay in power for 11 years, a period known in Peruvian politics as the *oncenio*. During this time he tried to forge what he called a 'new Fatherland'.

In common with other South American leaders, Leguía had woken up to the need to pay attention to new forces in Peruvian society. Up to now the workers, students, middle classes and Indians had been largely ignored. He thus began a programme of public works, building new railways, hospitals and schools, and promising to improve working conditions. Yet his policies still contained more familiar features of Peruvian governance, including a new rapprochement with the Catholic Church and a determined suppression of opposition. The economy, too, was still run on 'traditional' lines as Leguía encouraged the growth of both exports and imports. Public spending was largely funded by US investment, which was pouring into the country. This period in Peruvian history has been described as a 'sort of carnival for foreign capital' and one in which money was 'riotously squandered'. Apart from these investments, the Leguía regime displayed other signs of closeness with the US. Peru allowed Washington to arbitrate in the long-running territorial dispute with Chile (though the outcome, which backed a public referendum or plebiscite widely seen as favourable to Chile, was not to Lima's liking), while a number of Americans occupied key places in Peruvian ministries. The country even made 4 July a public holiday in honour of the US.[11]

The close links with America became politically damaging for Leguía, however. Many Peruvians were unhappy with the boundary agreement reached with Colombia over disputed jungle regions and many blamed US involvement. Some critics even claimed the country was effectively being governed from Washington. Nor could Leguía altogether silence those critics. One of the most prominent was Juan Carlos Mariátegui who, like Tristan Marof in Bolivia, believed his country's future lay in returning to the past and the collectivist lifestyle of the country's Indian communities. Another was the brilliant orator Víctor Raúl Haya de la Torre. Exiled in 1924, he created the created the American Revolutionary Popular Alliance (APRA in its Spanish initials) in Mexico, and later the APRA party in Peru itself. Haya de la Torre advocated state control of the economy and nationalisation, and championed not just the Indians and working classes but also Peru's middle classes. He was to remain an influential figure in Peruvian politics for many decades.

The onset of the Depression, and its rapid impact on Peru's import-export economy, combined with growing discontent over the influence of the US, spelt the end for Leguía. In 1930 he was deposed by a military coup and died later in prison. The new man in charge was an army officer, Luis Sánchez Cerro, who in 1931 beat the populist Haya de la Torre in a presidential election. APRA was furious, claiming their leader had been robbed of victory, and unrest mounted across the country, including a failed assassination attempt on the new president. In 1932 *Apristas*, as supporters of the party were called, staged an uprising in Trujillo. At the end of this failed revolt a number of military officers were executed, provoking even bloodier reprisals and guaranteeing bad relations between the army and APRA in the future. The spiral of violence culminated in 1933 when Sánchez Cerro was assassinated.

The rest of the decade was dominated by General Oscar Benavides. The new president adopted a paternalistic approach to government, carrying out public works, including a major road-building programme. Benavides, who stayed in power until 1939, also made some limited efforts to improve the lot of Indian communities and introduced legislation on retirement ages, pensions and sickness and disability. Yet the old tensions remained, and in 1936 an APRA-backed candidate won the election. Benavides's response was simply to annul the elections and carry on in power for another three years. His chosen successor was a banker and businessman Manuel Prado, whose government started to reduce the country's reliance on imports and exports. The regime was also noticeably more tolerant of opposition; there was a suspicion that Prado had done a deal with APRA under which in return for their not opposing his election, he would legalise them once he was in office. This he did, though not until the end of his term.

Prado's six years as president coincided with the Second World War. Before the war the Benavides regime had demonstrated some sympathies with the fascist governments in Italy and Spain; certainly his prime minister for a time, José de la Riva Agüero, was openly pro-fascist. However, Prado steered a pro-America and Allied course and broke off relations with the Axis Powers once Washington joined the war. Three years later Peru itself declared war. Surprisingly, given APRA's deep condemnation of American imperialism in previous years, Haya de la Torre largely supported Prado's stance. APRA was on something of a political journey, shedding much of its revolutionary rhetoric, and in 1945 the party backed the successful candidate José Luis Bustamente. Yet politics in Peru were still turbulent. Sections of the Apristas were angry at the movement's new stance, and with the help of a group of junior military officers tried to stage a rebellion.

Senior figures in the army responded by staging their own, successful, coup in 1948 with General Manuel Odría taking over the reins of power, backed by the traditional ruling upper classes. Haya de la Torre was forced to spend the next five years taking refuge in the Colombian Embassy in Lima. This new military dictatorship was to last for eight years. The country's politics would continue to follow a similarly turbulent course through much of the rest of the 20th century.

Francisco García Calderón's later career was to prove every bit as complicated and dramatic as the politics of his country. In 1920 he represented Peru at Geneva on the League of Nations but before long he was in open conflict with Leguía's regime in Lima. On 21 March 1921 García Calderón resigned as a representative of Peru and for the next decade flung himself more than ever into his writing, including an examination of contemporary German thinkers. It was not until after the fall of Leguía that García Calderón, who was still based in Paris, returned to the diplomatic fold and on 10 September 1930 once more became his country's official representative in the French capital. Three years later García Calderón was made his country's delegate to the League of Nations, and in 1938 he was asked to preside over the 103rd public session of the League's Council. However, he once again suffered from bouts of depression, as he had done after the death of his father, and his journalistic work was affected.

At the outbreak of the Second World War García Calderón stayed on as a diplomat in France, technically now accredited to the Vichy regime. But after Peru broke off relations with Germany in 1942 he was interned by the Nazis at an 'Ilag' camp at Bad Godesberg in Germany. 'Ilag' camps – the word is short for *Internierungslager* – were used to intern civilians from countries that were at war with Germany or any individuals considered to be enemies of the Third Reich. García Calderón's health was already in decline and the lack of proper medical care aggravated his condition. At the end of the war the Peruvian officially retired from the diplomatic service and in August 1947 Calderón and his wife returned to live in Peru, leaving Europe for good after 40 years.

García Calderón's mental health had deteriorated to such an extent that the following year he was admitted to the Víctor Larco Herrera mental hospital at Magdalena del Mar, Lima. The loss of his father, the death of his brother in the First World War and his internment during the Second World War had all taken their toll on the intellectual's state of mind. His and his wife's finances were also in a precarious state and in 1951 the country's Congress passed a resolution to increase his diplomatic pension – a sign of the esteem in which García Calderón was held by his fellow countrymen. He did not live much longer. On 1 July 1953 he died in the Peruvian capital, aged 70. His wife Rosa Amalia, helped by friends, later published some of his writings on Peru and the Americas posthumously. García Calderón's long and sometimes tragic career had finally come to an end.

Postscript

By any objective measurement, the four South American republics at the Peace Conference had little impact on events in Paris or the eventual Treaty of Versailles. Ecuador, Peru, Bolivia and Uruguay were invited to take part because they had shown solidarity with the Allies in the First World War, not because they were expected to play a significant role there.

The importance of the Peace Conference and Treaty for the four countries was, unsurprisingly then, limited. Paris did at least provide a rare occasion for these South American nations to be seen and occasionally heard on the world diplomatic stage. Probably the biggest beneficiary of the four in this respect was Uruguay. Its delegate Juan Antonio Buero clearly impressed the United States President Woodrow Wilson and his interventions helped underline Uruguay's modest but growing reputation as a country that, thanks to its small size and a lack of squabbles with neighbours, could operate as a kind of honest broker between rival Latin American countries. In this sense it was a South American version of Switzerland.

The delegates of the other three nations were no mere

anonymous bystanders either; Ecuador's Enrique Dorn y de Alsua, for example, showed considerable diplomatic skill and tenacity. However, Peru, Bolivia and Ecuador also brought parochial South American concerns to the Peace Conference – in Ecuador's case its problems with British bondholders and for Peru and Bolivia their land dispute with Chile – that were peripheral to the main proceedings and thus not calculated to make diplomats of the Great Powers well disposed towards them.

By far the most important outcome of the Peace Conference for the four nations was the creation of the League of Nations. Even here, though, the legacy is a mixed one. Peru, Bolivia, Ecuador and Uruguay all supported Woodrow Wilson's proposals for the League. But that organisation's usefulness to them was dramatically reduced once the United States decided not to join it, since it was hoped the League would provide a check on Washington's growing influence in the region. The League's failure even to attempt to sort out Bolivia and Peru's long-standing land dispute with Chile merely added to the feeling that the League was of limited use. It must be added, of course, that Ecuador did not help its cause in this respect by refusing to ratify the Treaty of Versailles – and thus join the League – for many years.

Ultimately the Paris Peace Conference, for all the fanfare and its high-minded ambition, could not change geographical and political reality for the South American nations. Whatever international conferences took place or global organisations existed, what mattered most to these countries was their relationship with their most immediate neighbours and, above all of course, their relationship with the United States.

Notes

1: Beginnings

1. Francisco García Calderón, *Les démocraties latines* (Flammarion, Paris: 1912) p 227, hereafter Calderón, *Les démocraties latines*; Francisco Garcia Calderón, *Latin America: Its Rise and Progress* (T F Unwin, London: 1913) pp 392–3; Leslie Bethell (ed), *Latin America: Economy and Society 1870–1930* (Cambridge University Press, Cambridge: 1989) p 276.

2. For an introduction to the complexity of this area, see Frederick B Pike, *The United States and the Andean Republics: Peru, Bolivia and Ecuador* (Harvard University Press, Cambridge, Massachusetts: 1977) pp 118–27, hereafter Pike, *Andean Republics*.

3. George Pendle, *Uruguay* (Oxford University Press, Oxford: 1963) p 24.

4. Frederick B Pike, *The Modern History of Peru* (Praeger, New York: 1967) p 24, hereafter Pike, *The Modern History of Peru*.

5. Ibid, p 115.

6. Pike, *Andean Republics,* p 98.

7. Ibid, p 155.

2: On the Eve of War

1. Pike, *Andean Republics,* p 154.

2. Hiram Bingham, *Across South America; an account of a journey from Buenos Aires to Lima by way of Potosí, with notes on Brazil, Argentina, Bolivia, Chile, and Peru* (Houghton Mifflin, Boston: 1911) p 338.

3. Percy Martin, *Peru of the Twentieth Century* (Edward Arnold, London: 1911) p 229; *New York Times,* 23 November 1913.

4. García Calderón, *Les démocraties latines,* pp 12–13.

5. Ibid, pp 292, 297.

6. Ibid, pp 329, 330.

7. Ibid, pp 298, 400.

8. *The Times,* 15 September 1919.

9. Ronn Pineo, *Ecuador and the United States: Useful Strangers* (The University of Georgia Press, Athens, Georgia: 2007) pp 72–84, hereafter Pineo, *Ecuador.*

10. Ibid, p 78.

11. Ibid, pp 68, 60–1, 88–91; *New York Times,* 15 December 1921.

12. Pike, *Andean Republics,* p 155.

13. *New York Times,* 26 May 1912.

14. Anne-Emanuelle Birn, 'Uruguay on the World Stage', *American Journal of Public Health,* Vol 95, No 9 (September 2005) pp 1509–10.

15. Georges Clemenceau, *South America To-Day: A Study Of Conditions, Social Political, And Commercial In Argentina, Uruguay And Brazil* (The Knickerbocker Press, London: 1911) pp 300, 308, 311.

3: The Republics and the War

1. *British Propaganda in Allied and Neutral Countries*, War Cabinet papers, January 1917, Cab/24/3.
2. Percy Martin, *Latin America and the War* (Johns Hopkins University Press, Baltimore: 1925) pp 269, 267, hereafter Martin, *Latin America and the War*.
3. Samuel Flagg Bemis, *The Latin American Policy of the United States* (Harcourt, New York: 1943) p 199.
4. Francisco García Calderón, *El Dilema de la Gran Guerra* (Ediciones Literarias, Paris: 1919) p v, hereafter Calderón, *El Dilema de la Gran Guerra*.
5. Martin, *Latin America and the War*, p 441.
6. Ibid, pp 445–6.
7. *The Times*, 15 September 1919.
8. Mendoza is a distant relative of the author's sister-in-law, whose family recounts the story.
9. *The Times*, 17 February 1916.
10. Pineo, *Ecuador*, p 82.
11. Martin, *Latin America and the War*, pp 352, 351.
12. Ibid, pp 363, 363–4.
13. Ibid, pp 76–7, 369, 78.
14. Ibid, p 391.
15. Pike, *Andean Republics*, p 165; *New York Times*, 19 November 1933.
16. Martin, *Latin America and the War*, p 455; *Le Temps*, 11 October 1917.
17. Ibid, pp 456–60.

4: Paris

1. *New York Times*, 30 November 1917.
2. Public Record Office, London (PRO): FO 608/174/2–6, p 262.

3. PRO: FO 608/174/2–6, p 262.
4. *The Times*, 28 November 1918.
5. *Archivo* Nacional del Ecuador, Quito; Legación del Ecuador, Paris 1919, p 1656.
6. Author interview with Dr Enrique J Buero, November 2008.
7. Ibid.
8. *Archivo* Nacional de Bolivia, Legación de Bolivia, Paris 1919, documents 144; 202.
9. PRO, Paris Peace Conference: FO 609/174/22.
10. *PRO,* Foreign Office Diplomatic logbook Quito, April 1919.
11. Author interview with Dr Enrique J Buero, November 2008.
12. Legación del Ecuador, Paris, 28 May 1919, documents 1789 and 1797.
13. PRO, Paris Peace Conference, Fo180.03601/1, p 451.
14. Ibid, p 452.
15. Ibid, pp 457, 460.
16. Ibid, pp 451, 463.
17. US National Archives, Foreign Relations of the United States (FRUS) memorandum, 21 March 1919.
18. Ibid.

5: The Treaty of Versailles and its Outcome

1. *Archivo* Nacional de Bolivia, Legación de Bolivia, Paris 1919, documents 196–8.
2. Legación de Bolivia, Paris 1919, documents 196–8; *Archivo* General de la Nación, Montevideo, Legación del Uruguay en Paris 1919, 3/919, p 3.
3. Archivo Nacional de Uruguay, Legación del Uruguay en Paris 1919, 3/919, p 2.

4. Legación del Uruguay en Paris 1919, 82/919; 94/919.
5. PRO, Fo207, British delegation letter, 28 April 1919.
6. *Diary of Edith Benham, Wilson Papers* Vol 58, p 187; Juan A Buero Harley, the delegate's grandson, was kind enough to send the author a copy of the note.
7. Legación del Uruguay en Paris 1919, 9067.
8. Legación del Uruguay en Paris 1919, telegrams 827/2.
9. Conference de Paix secretariat memo, 1 April 1919.
10. Calderón, *El Dilema de la Gran Guerra,* pp vii, 290–1.
11. Legación de Bolivia, Paris 1919, document 203.
12. PRO, FO 608/173/30.
13. Legación de Bolivia, Paris 1919, document 198.
14. Author interview with Dr Enrique J Buero, November 2008; Margaret MacMillan, *Paris 1919: Six Months that Changed the World* (Random House, New York: 2001) p 477.
15. Legación del Ecuador, document 2346, 16 July 1919.

6: The League of Nations

1. Elmer Bendiner, *A Time for Angels – the tragicomic history of the League of Nations* (New York: Knopf, 1975) pp 23–4.
2. Calderón, *Les démocraties latines*, pp 295–300.
3. Jorge Gumucio Granier, *United States and the Bolivian Seacoast* (published online, 1996, at: http://www.boliviaweb.com/mar/sea), Chapter 6, hereafter Granier, *United States and the Bolivian Seacoast.*
4. Legación de Bolivia, Paris 1919, document 81, 14 December 1918.
5. Granier, *United States and the Bolivian Seacoast,* Chapter 6; Ronald Bruce St John, *The Foreign Policy of*

Peru (Lynne Rienner, Boulder: 1992) p 160, hereafter St John, *The Foreign Policy of Peru*.

6. Legación del Ecuador, Paris 1919, document 2489, 11 September 1919.

7. J Lloyd Mecham, *A Survey of United States-Latin American Relations* (Houghton Mifflin, Atlanta: 1965) p 103, hereafter Lloyd Mecham, *A Survey of United States-Latin American Relations*; Bendiner, *A Time for Angels*, pp 163–4.

8. Granier, *United States and the Bolivian Seacoast*, Chapter 8.

9. Bendiner, *A Time for Angels*, pp 317–20.

10. *El Plata, Uruguay*, 7 March 1923.

11. *New York Times*, 23 July 1922.

12. PRO, FO 2719/6458, Peace Conference correspondence.

7: Revolution and Nationalism

1. Pike, *Andean Republics*, p 187; *The Times*, 7 September 1920.

2. Pineo, *Ecuador*, p 117.

3. Published in the house journal of the association for Ecuador's Foreign Ministry employees, the Asociación de Funcionarios y Empleados del Servicio Exterior Ecuatoriano, and available online at http://www.afese. com/img/revistas/revista25/jeancontoux.pdf

4. *The Times*, 17 November 1919.

5. *La Razón*, 30 April 1925.

6. *El Diario*, 31 July 1930.

7. Lloyd Mecham, *A Survey of United States-Latin American Relations*, pp 117–18.

8. Pike, *Andean Republics*, p 171; see also *The Times*, 24 August 1920.

Chronology

YEAR	THE LIVES AND THE LANDS
1821	Peru proclaims independence from Spain.
1825	Bolivia proclaimed an independent state.
1828	Uruguay becomes an independent state.
1830	Ecuador becomes a fully independent state.
1845	Enrique Dorn y de Alsua born. Ecuador: President General Juan José Flores goes into exile after civil war.
1859	Ecuador suffers 'Terrible Year' of anarchy, revolts and separatist movements.
1861	5 Oct: Ismael Montes Gamboa born, La Paz, Bolivia.
1875	Ecuador: Conservative president Gabriel García Moreno hacked to death.
1879	Outbreak of War of the Pacific involving Bolivia, Peru and Chile; Montes joins up to fight with fellow Bolivians. Peru loses Tacna and Arica. As a result of the war Bolivia loses its Pacific coastline.
1883	8 Apr: Francisco García Calderón born, Valparaiso, Chile, where his father was in temporary detention as a result of the War of the Pacific.

YEAR	HISTORY	CULTURE
1821	Death of Napoleon.	Walter Scott, *Kenilworth*.
1825	Portugal recognises Brazilian independence.	The Diaries of Samuel Pepys first published.
1828	Russia declares war on Turkey.	Alexandre Dumas, *The Three Musketeers*.
1830	Revolution in Paris: Louis Philippe becomes King.	Stendahl, *Le Rouge et Le Noir*.
1845	First Sikh War begins. First submarine telegraph cable laid across English Channel.	Benjamin Disraeli, *Sybil*. Edgar Allen Poe, *The Raven, and Other Poems*.
1859	Franco-Austrian War. Future German Kaiser Wilhelm II born.	Charles Dickens, *A Tale of Two Cities*.
1861	Outbreak of American Civil War.	George Eliot, *Silas Marner*.
1875	Risings in Bosnia and Herzegovina against Turkish rule.	Mark Twain, *The Adventures of Tom Sawyer*.
1879	Zulu War. Alsace-Lorraine declared integral part of Germany.	Henry James, *Daisy Miller*. Peter Tchaikovsky, *Eugene Onegin*.
1883	French gain control of Tunis. British decide to evacuate the Sudan. Orient Express (Paris–Constantinople) makes first run.	Richard Wagner dies. Friedrich Nietzsche, *Thus Spake Zarathustra*.

YEAR	THE LIVES AND THE LANDS
1886	Bolivia: Montes becomes a barrister.
1888	Uruguay: Juan Antonio Buero is born in Paris.
1889	First International Conference of American States.
	Dorn helps organise Ecuador's representation at Paris Universal Exhibition.
1894	Bolivia: Montes becomes a Member of Parliament.
1895	Ecuador: Liberals seize power under José Eloy Alfaro Delgado.
1899	Bolivia: Liberals seize power. Montes becomes War Minister.
1901	Peru: Calderón enters San Marco university in Lima where he becomes part of a small group of talented young intellectuals.
1902	Dorn becomes secretary of the Ecuadorian Legation in Paris.
1903	Uruguay: José Batlle y Ordóñez starts the first of two four-year terms as president that will see his country develop the first welfare state in Latin America.
	Bolivia: After a short conflict, Bolivia cedes land to Brazil under Treaty of Petrópolis.

YEAR	HISTORY	CULTURE
1886	Canadian-Pacific Railway completed.	Karl Marx's *Das Kapital* published in English.
1888	Kaiser Wilhelm II accedes to German throne.	Vincent Van Gogh, *The Yellow Chair*.
1889	Austro-Hungarian Crown Prince Rudolf commits suicide at Mayerling. London Dock Strike.	Jerome K Jerome, *Three Men in a Boat*. Richard Strauss, *Don Juan*.
1894	Sino-Japanese War. Dreyfus Case begins in France.	Anthony Hope, *The Prisoner of Zenda*.
1895	Cuba rebels against Spanish rule.	H G Wells, *The Time Machine*.
1899	First Peace Conference at the Hague.	Arthur Pinero, *Trelawny of the Wells*.
1901	US President William McKinley assassinated: Theodore Roosevelt succeeds him. First transatlantic radio signal transmitted.	Nobel Prize in Literature: Sully Prudhomme (France). Pablo Picasso's 'Blue Period' begins.
1902	USA acquires perpetual control over Panama Canal.	Nobel Prize in Literature: Theodor Mommsen (Germany). Edward Elgar, *Pomp and Circumstance March No 1*.
1903	Beginning of Entente Cordiale: King Edward VII of Britain visits Paris, French President Loubet visits London. Wright Brothers' first flight.	Nobel Prize in Literature: B Bjørnson (Norway). Henry James, *The Ambassadors*. Film: *The Great Train Robbery*.

YEAR	THE LIVES AND THE LANDS
1904	Peru: Calderón starts work as a journalist. Bolivia: Montes becomes president for the first time. Bolivia formally cedes land to Chile in return for a new railway line from Arica to La Paz.
1905	Peru: Calderón plunges into depression after the death of his father.
1906	Peru: Calderón and his three brothers move to Paris to start a new life in Europe. Calderón is made Chancellor at the Peruvian legation.
1908	Uruguay: Buero helps organise the first Congress of American Students in Montevideo. Ecuador: The Guayaquil and Quito Railway is opened.
1909	Bolivia: Montes steps down as president, and becomes the country's representative in Britain and France. Peru: Calderón becomes Second Secretary at the Peruvian legation in Paris.

YEAR	HISTORY	CULTURE
1904	Entente Cordiale settles British-French colonial differences.	Nobel Prize in Literature: Frédéric Mistral (France), J Echegaray y Eizaguirre (Spain).
	Russo-Japanese War begins.	J M Barrie, *Peter Pan*.
	Theodore Roosevelt elected US President.	Giacomo Puccini, *Madame Butterfly*.
	Photoelectric cell invented.	
1905	'Bloody Sunday': police break-up Russian demonstration.	Nobel Prize in Literature: H Sieniewicz (Poland).
	Tsar Nicholas II issues the 'October Manifesto'.	E M Forster, *Where Angels Fear to Tread*.
1906	Britain grants self-government to Transvaal and Orange River Colonies.	Nobel Prize in Literature: Giosue Carducci (Italy).
	Major earthquake in San Francisco USA kills over 1,000.	Edward Dent founds *Everyman's Library*.
1908	*The Daily Telegraph* publishes German Kaiser Wilhelm II's hostile remarks towards England.	Nobel Prize in Literature: Rudolf Eucken (Germany).
	William Howard Taft elected US President.	Kenneth Grahame, *The Wind in the Willows*.
1909	Britain's Edward VII makes state visits to Berlin and Rome.	Nobel Prize in Literature: Selma Lagerlöf (Sweden).
	Anglo-German discussions on control of Baghdad railway.	H G Wells, *Tono-Bungay*.
	Turkish nationalists force Kiamil Pasha, Grand Vizier of Turkey, to resign.	Vasily Kandinsky paints first abstract paintings.

YEAR	THE LIVES AND THE LANDS
1910	Uruguay: Buero becomes professor of international law at both the Commercial High School and the School of Law and Social Sciences in Montevideo.
1912	Peru: Calderón publishes *Les democraties latines de l'Amerique* on Latin America and democracy, with a foreword from French Prime Minister Raymond Poincaré.
1913	Bolivia: Montes becomes president for the second time. Uruguay: Buero joins Foreign Ministry in Montevideo and later becomes an MP.
1914	Ecuador, Bolivia and Uruguay declare themselves neutral at start of war in Europe; Peru makes no such formal declaration but acts in accordance with neutral status. Peru: Colonel Oscar Benavides becomes president. Nov: Ecuador: Britain and France protest after the German cruiser *Leipzig* refuels at the Galapagos, and asks America to intervene. Ecuador confirms its neutrality.
1915	Ecuador: Dispute with British bondholders and the United States government over the Guayaquil and Quito Railway.
1916	5 May: Calderón's brother José killed at Verdun.

YEAR	HISTORY	CULTURE
1910	Britain's King Edward VII dies; succeeded by George V. Liberals win British General Election.	Nobel Prize in Literature: Paul von Heyse (Germany). E M Forster, *Howard's End*. R Vaughan Williams, *Sea Symphony*.
1912	*Titanic* sinks: 1,513 die. First Balkan War begins. Woodrow Wilson elected US President.	C G Jung, *The Theory of Psychoanalysis*. Maurice Ravel, *Daphne et Chloe*.
1913	London Ambassadors Conference ends First Balkan War. Second Balkan War begins and ends. US Federal Reserve System established.	Nobel Prize in Literature: Sir R Tagore (India). Nobel Prize in Literature: Gerhart Hauptmann (Germany). Thomas Mann, *Death in Venice*.
1914	Archduke Franz Ferdinand of Austria-Hungary and wife assassinated in Sarajevo. First World War begins: Battles of Mons, the Marne and First Ypres; trench warfare on Western Front; Russians defeated in Battles of Tannenberg and Masurian Lakes.	Nobel Prize in Literature: No award. James Joyce, *Dubliners*. Theodore Dreiser, *The Titan*. Gustav Holst, *The Planets*. Matisse, *The Red Studio*. Georges Braque, *Music*. Film: Charlie Chaplin in *Making a Living*.
1915	First World War: Battles of Neuve Chapelle and Loos. Germans sink British liner *Lusitania,* killing 1,198.	Nobel Prize in Literature: Romain Rolland (France). John Buchan, *The Thirty-Nine Steps*.
1916	First World War: Battles of Verdun, the Somme and Jutland. US President Woodrow Wilson re-elected.	Nobel Prize in Literature: V von Heidenstam (Sweden). Film: *Intolerance*.

YEAR	THE LIVES AND THE LANDS
1917	Germany declares unrestricted submarine warfare to blockade Britain, Italy and France, thereby blocking shipping from South American countries.
	6 Apr: America declares war on Germany.
	13 Apr: Bolivia formally breaks off relations with Germany.
	Oct: Peru and Uruguay formally break off relations with Germany.
	Nov: Montes ends his second and final term as president of Bolivia.
	Dec: Ecuador formally breaks off relations with Germany.
1918	Apr: British Special Mission on trade to South America.
	Peru: Calderón named minister in France.
	Uruguay: Buero becomes interim Foreign Minister and later Industry Minister.
	Bolivia: Montes becomes minister to London and Paris.

YEAR	HISTORY	CULTURE
1917	First World War: Battle of Passchendaele (Third Ypres); British and Commonwealth forces take Jerusalem. February Revolution in Russia. Balfour Declaration favouring establishment of national home for Jewish People in Palestine. German and Russian delegates sign armistice at Brest-Litovsk.	Nobel Prize in Literature: Karl Gjellerup & H Pontoppidan (Denmark). P G Wodehouse, *The Man With Two Left Feet.* T S Eliot, *Prufrock and Other Observations.* Film: *Easy Street.*
1918	First World War: Peace Treaty of Brest-Litovsk signed between Russia and Central Powers; German Spring offensives on Western Front fail; Allied offensives on Western Front have German army in full retreat; Armistice signed between Allies and Germany; German Fleet surrenders.	Nobel Prize in Literature: No award. Luigi Pirandello, *Six Characters in Search of an Author.* Bela Bartok, *Bluebeard's Castle.* Giacomo Puccini, *Il Trittico.*

YEAR	THE LIVES AND THE LANDS
1919	Ecuador: Dorn y de Alsua, his country's minister in France, is chosen as delegate to Paris Peace Conference.
	Bolivia: Montes, now his country's representative in France, is chosen to be delegate to the Paris Peace Conference.
	Peru: Calderón, now minister in Brussels, is named as one of three alternating delegates at the Paris Peace Conference, with diplomats Carlos Candamo and Victor Manuel Maurtua.
	Uruguay: Buero is chosen as one of Uruguay's representatives at the Paris Peace Conference, along with Juan Carlos Blanco and Jacobo Varela Acevedo.
	Ecuador: Alsua becomes first Ecuadorian member of International Olympic Committee.
	Mar: Buero is named Minister of Foreign Affairs, under prime minister Brum, but remains at the Peace Conference.
	28 Apr: League of Nations Covenant is passed.
	Jun: Peru: Calderón publishes *El Dilemma de la Gran Guerra*.
	Jul: Peru: Start of 11-year rule or *oncenio* of Augusto Leguía.
	Uruguay: Buero discusses bilateral Arbitration Treaty with United States delegate Robert Lansing. It eventually comes to nothing.
	Uruguay: A new constitution comes into force, with an Executive Council handling domestic issues.
1920	Bolivia: Republican Party seizes power. Montes is disowned as his country's representative in Paris.
	Peru: Calderón becomes a Peruvian representative at the League of Nations.
1921	11 Mar: Calderón resigns as Peruvian representative in Europe in protest at Leguía regime.

YEAR	HISTORY	CULTURE
1919	Communist Revolt in Berlin.	Nobel Prize in Literature: Carl Spitteler (Switzerland).
	Benito Mussolini founds Fascist movement in Italy.	Bauhaus movement founded by Walter Gropius.
	Britain and France authorise resumption of commercial relations with Germany.	Vasily Kandinsky, *Dreamy Improvisation*.
	British-Persian agreement at Tehran to preserve integrity of Persia.	Paul Klee, *Dream Birds*.
		Thomas Hardy, *Collected Poems*.
	Irish War of Independence begins.	Herman Hesse, *Demian*.
	US Senate vetoes ratification of Versailles Treaty leaving US outside League of Nations.	George Bernard Shaw, *Heartbreak House*.
		Eugene D'Albert, *Revolutionshochzeit*.
		Edward Elgar, *Concerto in E Minor for Cello*.
		Manuel de Falla, *The Three-Cornered Hat*.
		Film: *The Cabinet of Dr Caligari*.
1920	League of Nations comes into existence.	Nobel Prize in Literature: Knut Hamsun (Norway).
	The Hague selected as seat of International Court of Justice.	F Scott Fitzgerald, *This Side of Paradise*.
	League of Nations headquarters moves to Geneva.	Franz Kafka, *The Country Doctor*.
	Warren G Harding wins US Presidential election.	Katherine Mansfield, *Bliss*.
1921	Peace treaty signed between Russia and Germany.	Nobel Prize in Literature: Anatole France (France).
	Washington Naval Treaty signed.	D H Lawrence, *Women in Love*.

YEAR	THE LIVES AND THE LANDS
1923	Uruguay is elected to League of Nations Council. Blanco becomes the country's representative.
1925	Ecuador: Liberals deposed by military coup; military later hand power to Isidro Ayora, but he is removed by another coup in 1931. A period of political instability follows. Uruguay: Buero becomes president of the Senate.
1930	Peru: After the fall of Leguía regime, Calderón is named the country's representative in France. First football world cup is held in, and won by, Uruguay. Bolivia: Montes returns to La Paz after of exile and briefly becomes vice-president.
1932	Bolivia starts disastrous Chaco War with Paraguay. At its end in 1935 Bolivia surrenders 50,000 square miles of land.

YEAR	HISTORY	CULTURE
1923	French and Belgian troops occupy the Ruhr when Germany fails to make reparation payments.	Nobel Prize in Literature: W B Yeats (Ireland). P G Wodehouse, *The Inimitable Jeeves*.
1925	Mussolini announces he will take dictatorial powers in Italy. British Pound Sterling returns to Gold Standard. Paul von Hindenburg elected President of Germany. Locarno Treaty signed in London.	Nobel Prize in Literature: George Bernard Shaw (Ireland). Noel Coward, *Hay Fever*. Franz Kafka, *The Trial*. Virginia Woolf, *Mrs Dalloway*. Pablo Picasso, *Three Dancers*. Film: *Battleship Potemkin*.
1930	Britain, France, Italy, Japan and US sign London Naval Treaty regulating naval expansion. British Imperial Conference held in London: Statute of Westminster approved.	Nobel Prize in Literature: Sinclair Lewis (USA). W H Auden, *Poems*. Noel Coward, *Private Lives*. Max Beckmann, *Self-portrait with a Saxophone*. Film: *All Quiet on the Western Front*.
1932	Germany withdraws temporarily from Geneva Disarmament Conference demanding permission for armaments equal to those of other powers. Franklin D Roosevelt wins US Presidential election.	Nobel Prize in Literature: John Galsworthy (Great Britain). Aldous Huxley, *Brave New World*. Sergei Prokofiev, *Piano Concerto No. 5 in G major Op. 55*.

YEAR	THE LIVES AND THE LANDS
1933	16 Oct: Bolivia: Montes dies in La Paz, aged 72. Peru: Calderón is again made representative at the League of Nations. Uruguay: President Gabriel Terra stages bloodless coup and dissolves the government's National Council. Buero's brother-in-law, former president Balthasar Brum, commits suicide in protest.
1934	Ecuador: Dorn's name is linked with Stavisky scandal that rocks French Establishment. Ecuador ratifies Treaty of Versailles and finally joins the League of Nations.
1935	Uruguay: Buero joins Permanent Court of Arbitration in The Hague.
1936	May: Bolivia Military coup ushers in period of government run by military veterans of Chaco War.
1941	Ecuador is defeated in war with Peru, and loses territory as a result.

YEAR	HISTORY	CULTURE
1933	Kurt von Schleicher falls; Adolf Hitler appointed Chancellor of Germany. Japan announces it will leave League of Nations. Geneva Disarmament Conference collapses. Germany withdraws from League of Nations and Disarmament Conference.	Nobel Prize in Literature: Ivan Bunin (USSR). George Orwell, *Down and Out in Paris and London*. Henri Matisse, *The Dance*. Richard Strauss, *Arabella*. Duke Ellington's Orchestra debuts in Britain. Films: *Duck Soup. King Kong. Queen Christina*.
1934	Germany: 'Night of the Long Knives'; role of German President and Chancellor merged, Hitler becomes *Führer* after German President Paul von Hindenburg dies. USSR admitted to League of Nations.	Nobel Prize in Literature: Luigi Pirandello (Italy). Robert Graves, *I, Claudius*. Dmitri Shostakovich, *Lady Macbeth of Mtsensk*. Film: *David Copperfield*.
1935	League of Nations imposes sanctions against Italy following invasion of Abyssinia.	Nobel Prize in Literature: No award. Films: *The 39 Steps. Top Hat*.
1936	German troops occupy Rhineland. Outbreak of Spanish Civil War.	Nobel Prize in Literature: Eugene O'Neill (USA). Penguin Books starts paperback revolution. Berlin Olympics.
1941	Second World War: Germany invades USSR. Japan attacks Pearl Harbor; Germany and Italy declare war on USA.	Noel Coward, *Blithe Spirit*. Films: *Citizen Kane. Dumbo. The Maltese Falcon*.

YEAR	THE LIVES AND THE LANDS
1942	Jan: Ecuador, Bolivia, Uruguay and Peru sever diplomatic links with Germany. Dec: Bolivia: Massacre of miners at Catavi. Peru: Calderón is interned by Germans at camp near Bonn.
1943	Apr: Bolivia declares war on Germany and Japan.
1945	Feb: Peru and Uruguay declare war on Germany and Japan. Peru: At the end of the war, Calderón retires from diplomatic service.
1946	Bolivian leader Major Gaulberto Villarroel is publicly lynched on the streets of La Paz.
1947	Peru: Calderón leaves France for the last time and returns home.

YEAR	HISTORY	CULTURE
1942	Second World War: Rommel retakes Tobruk; later defeated at El Alamein. US invasion of Guadalcanal turns Japanese tide. Battle of Stalingrad in USSR.	Nobel Prize in Literature: No award. Dmitri Shostakovich, *Symphony No. 7.* Films: *Casablanca. How Green was my Valley.*
1943	Second World War: Italy surrenders unconditionally. Tehran Conference: Churchill, Roosevelt and Stalin meet.	Nobel Prize in Literature: No award. Richard Rogers and Oscar Hammerstein, *Oklahoma!*
1945	Second World War: Hitler commits suicide in Berlin; city surrenders to Soviets. VE Day: 8 May. US drops atomic bombs on Hiroshima and Nagasaki: Japan surrenders to Allies.	Nobel Prize in Literature: Gabriela Mistralo (Chile). Karl Popper, *The Open Society and its Enemies.* George Orwell, *Animal Farm.* Evelyn Waugh, *Brideshead Revisited.* Film: *Brief Encounter.*
1946	Churchill declares Stalin has lowered 'Iron Curtain' across Europe, signalling formal start of Cold War.	Nobel Prize in Literature: Hermann Hesse (Switzerland). Bertrand Russell, *History of Western Philosophy.* Films: *Great Expectations. It's a Wonderful Life.*
1947	US Secretary of State George C Marshall calls for relief aid to Europe. Indian Independence and Partition.	Nobel Prize in Literature: André Gide (France). Albert Camus, *The Plague.* Anne Frank, *The Diary of Anne Frank.*

YEAR	THE LIVES AND THE LANDS
1948	Peru: Calderón is admitted to a mental institution suffering from depression.
1950	5 Jun: Uruguay: Buero dies, aged 62.
1951	Peru: Peruvian Congress votes to increase the pension of a now impecunious Calderón.
1953	1 Jul: Peru: Calderón dies at age of 70.

YEAR	HISTORY	CULTURE
1948	Israel established as independent state: recognised by US and USSR. Western Allies organise Berlin Airlift after USSR blockades Berlin.	Nobel Prize in Literature: T S Eliot (Great Britain). Graham Greene, *The Heart of the Matter*. London Olympics.
1950	Korean War breaks out.	Nobel Prize in Literature: Bertrand Russell (Great Britain). Film: *Rashomon*.
1951	Korean War: Chinese forces take Seoul. Juan Peron re-elected President of Argentina.	Nobel Prize in Literature: Pär F Lagerkvist (Swedish). Isaac Asimov, *Foundation*.
1953	Korean Armistice signed.	Dmitri Shostakovich, *Symphony No. 10*.

Further Reading

Bolivia, Ecuador, Peru and Uruguay

There is no shortage of general histories about South America in general and these four countries in particular. For a very general, brief outline from pre-colonial times to the middle of the 20th century, George Pendle's A *History of Latin America* (Penguin: 1969) is still a valuable read. The best detailed survey of the colonial history of the region and then independence up to the second half of the 18th century remains the *Cambridge History of Latin America* volumes I–III (Cambridge: 1985), edited by Leslie Bethell. For a detailed and authoritative account of the South American wars of independence see *The Spanish American Revolutions 1808–1826* (Norton: 1986) by John Lynch. *Latin America, Economy and Society 1870–1930* (Cambridge: 1989), edited by Leslie Bethell, provides a fascinating insight into the period, though it is not light reading. A more accessible and more general history can be found in *Modern Latin America* (Oxford: 1988) by Thomas E Skidmore and Peter H Smith.

For a history of Bolivia, the best general history in English is Herbert S Klein's *A Concise History of Bolivia* (Cambridge: 2003). An older but still relevant work is *Bolivia:*

Land, Location and Politics since 1825 (Cambridge: 1972) by J Valerie Fisher. And though its primary focus is on foreign relations, *The United States and the Andean Republics, Peru, Bolivia and Ecuador* (Harvard: 1977) by Frederick B Pike also discusses domestic politics and trends.

For Ecuador the choice is rather more limited. Pike's book on the Andean Republics contains the country's domestic history, as does Ronn Pineo's *Ecuador and the United States: Useful Stranger* (University of Georgia: 2006). The most comprehensive work in English on Ecuadorian domestic history, however, is probably David W Schodt's *Ecuador: An Andean Enigma* (Westview: 1987).

For Peru the best single-volume history in English is probably still Frederick B Pike's *The Modern History of Peru* (Praeger: 1967). Again, his work on *The United States and the Andean Republics* is also useful for domestic affairs. *Modern Latin America*, mentioned earlier, also has a chapter devoted to Peru.

Works on Uruguayan history in English have, understandably perhaps, focused on the extraordinary political achievements of the creator of modern Uruguay, José Batlle y Ordoñez. For a detailed read see Milton I Vanger's trilogy of biographical studies on Batlle. The first is *José Batlle y Ordoñez of Uruguay: The Creator of His Times, 1902–1907* (Harvard: 1963), the second is *The Model Country: José Batlle y Ordoñez of Uruguay, 1907–1915* (Brandeis: 1980) and the final one *Uruguay's Jose Batlle y Ordonez: The Determined Visionary, 1915–1917* (Lynne Rienner: 2009). For a very brief and now admittedly somewhat dated introductory history, see George Pendle's *Uruguay* (Oxford: 1963).

Foreign relations

On foreign relations, a valuable book in relation to Uruguay is *The United States and the Southern Cone: Argentina, Chile, and Uruguay* (Harvard: 1976) by Arthur Preston Whitaker. Pike's *The United States and the Andean Republics, Peru, Bolivia and Ecuador* (Harvard: 1977) is still one of the most important books on the subject for the three Andean Republics. For Peru there is also Ronald Bruce St John's *The Foreign Policy of Peru* (Lynne Rienner: 1992) which starts from independence and covers the topic through to the start of the 1990s. On Peru's relations with America, *Peru and the United States 1900–1962* (University of Notre Dame: 1964) by James C Carey is an older but still useful work. For a general work covering America and Latin America, J Lloyd Mecham's *A Survey of United States-Latin American Relations* (Houghton Mifflin: 1965) is an insightful read, though it sees the relationship very much from an American point of view.

South America, the Paris Peace Conference and the Treaty of Versailles

It has to be stated from the outset that outside national government archives, specific material on the South American countries, the Paris Peace Conference and the Treaty of Versailles is hard to come by. However, in addition to the above titles there are some works that deal with the war and events immediately afterwards. The most useful is still Percy Martin's *Latin America and the War* (Johns Hopkins: 1925), which despite its age and the fact that it is sometimes a little uncritical is still a marvellous survey of how the nations of Latin America responded to the war. *South America and the First World War* (Cambridge: 1988) by Bill Albert, meanwhile, charts the economic impact of the war on Brazil, Argentina, Peru and Chile. As its title suggests, *The Aftermath of War: World War I and US Policy Toward Latin America* (New York University Press: 1971) by Joseph L Tulchin covers the end of the war and the years immediately afterwards.

An excellent and concise introduction to the Conference is Alan Sharp's *The Versailles Settlement: Peacemaking in Paris, 1919* (Macmillan: 1991; second edition 2008). A lengthier account is Margaret MacMillan's compelling *Paris 1919: Six months that changed the world* (Random House: 2001), which manages to capture the mood of the city at the time of the Conference as well as the negotiations themselves. Lord Riddell's *Intimate Diary of the Peace Conference and After 1918–1923* (Victor Gollancz: 1933) is an account of someone who was on the fringes of the Conference, but who was in regular contact with the British delegation, including Lloyd George. An insider's view from an American perspective can be found in *What Really happened at Paris: The Story of the Peace Conference 1918–1919* (Charles Scribner: 1921) by Edward Mandell House and Charles Seymour. Excerpts of writings from historians and politicians concerning the Conference and the subsequent Treaty are contained in *The Treaty of Versailles* (Greenhaven: 2001) edited by Jeff Hay. Analysis of the peace process from an American viewpoint is found in *Woodrow Wilson and the Paris Peace Conference* (D C Heath: 1972) edited by N Gordon Levin, Jr. Thomas A Bailey's *Woodrow Wilson and The Lost Peace* (Macmillan: 1944) examines the role of Wilson and also American public opinion. *A Time for Angels – the tragicomic history of the League of Nations* (Knopf: 1975) by Elmer Bendiner is a lively account of the creation and ultimately the demise of the League of Nations.

Picture Sources

The author and publishers wish to express their thanks to the following sources of illustrative material and/or permission to reproduce it. They will make proper acknowledgements in future editions in the event that any omissions have occurred.

Corbis.

Endpapers
The Signing of Peace in the Hall of Mirrors, Versailles, 28th June 1919 by Sir William Orpen (Imperial War Museum: akg-images)
Front row: Dr Johannes Bell (Germany) signing with Herr Hermann Müller leaning over him
Middle row (seated, left to right): General Tasker H Bliss, Col E M House, Mr Henry White, Mr Robert Lansing, President Woodrow Wilson (United States); M Georges Clemenceau (France); Mr David Lloyd George, Mr Andrew Bonar Law, Mr Arthur J Balfour, Viscount Milner, Mr G N Barnes (Great Britain); Prince Saionji (Japan)
Back row (left to right): M Eleftherios Venizelos (Greece);

Dr Afonso Costa (Portugal); Lord Riddell (British Press); Sir George E Foster (Canada); M Nikola Pašić (Serbia); M Stephen Pichon (France); Col Sir Maurice Hankey, Mr Edwin S Montagu (Great Britain); the Maharajah of Bikaner (India); Signor Vittorio Emanuele Orlando (Italy); M Paul Hymans (Belgium); General Louis Botha (South Africa); Mr W M Hughes (Australia)

Jacket images

(Front): Imperial War Museum: akg Images.

(Back): *Peace Conference at the Quai d'Orsay* by Sir William Orpen (Imperial War Museum: akg Images).

Left to right (seated): Signor Orlando (Italy); Mr Robert Lansing, President Woodrow Wilson (United States); M Georges Clemenceau (France); Mr David Lloyd George, Mr Andrew Bonar Law, Mr Arthur J Balfour (Great Britain); Left to right (standing): M Paul Hymans (Belgium); Mr Eleftherios Venizelos (Greece); The Emir Feisal (The Hashemite Kingdom); Mr W F Massey (New Zealand); General Jan Smuts (South Africa); Col E M House (United States); General Louis Botha (South Africa); Prince Saionji (Japan); Mr W M Hughes (Australia); Sir Robert Borden (Canada); Mr G N Barnes (Great Britain); M Ignacy Paderewski (Poland)

Index

Makers of the Modern World

UK PUBLICATION: November 2008 to December 2010
CLASSIFICATION: Biography/History/
    International Relations
FORMAT: 198 × 128mm
EXTENT: 208pp
ILLUSTRATIONS: 6 photographs plus 4 maps
TERRITORY: world

Chronology of life in context, full index, bibliography innovative layout
with sidebars